There's a Word for It

There's a Word for It

The Explosion

of the

American Language Since 1900

Sol Steinmetz

Harmony Books

NEW YORK

Copyright © 2010 by Sol Steinmetz

Published in the United States by Harmony Books,
an imprint of the Crown Publishing Group,
a division of Random House, Inc., New York.
www.crownpublishing.com

Harmony Books is a registered trademark and the Harmony Books
colophon is a trademark of Random House, Inc.

Library of Congress Cataloging-in-Publication Data

Steinmetz, Sol.
There's a word for it: the explosion of the English language
since 1900 / Sol Steinmetz.—1st ed.
p. cm.
Includes bibliographical references and index.
1. English language—United States—Lexicology.   2. English
language—United States—New words.   3. English language—
Social aspects—United States.   4. Language and culture—
United States.   I. Title.
PE2830.S65 2010
423'.028—dc22
2009034943

ISBN 978-0-375-42617-9

Printed in the United States of America

Design by *Lynne Amft*

1 3 5 7 9 10 8 6 4 2

First Edition

To Tzippie, with love

Contents

Introduction

Why This Book

The idea for this book developed in the late 1990s, as I was writing the essay "Defining Our Language for the 21st Century" for the 1997 Edition of the *Random House Webster's College Dictionary*. In that essay I tried to show how every decade since the 1940s has left its stamp on the English language. I surveyed the new vocabulary of each decade and listed a selection of words that reflected the decade's peculiar character. For example, under the heading "New Words of the 1940s" I listed a group of terms beginning with *A-bomb* and ending with *zip gun* and *zonk*.

After writing the essay, I continued to collect new vocabulary to keep up with the expansion of English. As I wrote in the essay, "Judging by its present rate of expansion, the English vocabulary is likely to continue its vigorous growth during the next century. The world-wide influence of English, reinforced by electronic communication, will develop further what has been already called 'World English,' an international language whose ever-growing vocabulary derives from a rich mixture of native stock and foreign borrowings."

Since 1900 every decade has contributed a substantial number of new words to the English vocabulary. If we tackle each decade, we may discover a pattern that reflects the character and historical nature of the decade.

A Typical Decade: 1920–29

Almost five thousand new words were absorbed into English between 1920 and 1929. Among them were such terms as *Dada* and *Dadaism, Fascism* and *Fascist, hijack* (v.), *id, leotard, mastectomy, motel, nonviolence, penicillin, scofflaw, superego, totalitarian* and *totalitarianism,* and *zipper.* The list evokes a sense of the cultural, social, and political atmosphere of that decade.

Dada and *Dadaism* came into English from French in 1920 to challenge the conventional art world; *Fascism* and *Fascist* came from Italian in 1921 as precursors of the Nazi era; *hijack* surfaced in 1923 from the language of rumrunners during Prohibition; the *id* was a Freudian term that entered the language in 1924 along with *ego* and *superego*; *leotard* came in 1920 from the name of a French trapeze artist who wore the skintight garment; *mastectomy* was first recorded in 1923 in *Stedman's Medical Dictionary*; *motel* was coined in 1925 from "motor hotel" by a company that planned to build a chain of such roadside inns; *nonviolence* appeared in 1920 and was attributed to the Hindu nationalist leader Gandhi; *penicillin* was coined by its discoverer, Alexander Fleming, in 1929; *scofflaw* was a winning word in a 1924 contest to describe a person who breaks the law by drinking liquor illegally (remember, this was Prohibition); *totalitarian* and *totalitarianism* came in 1926 from Italian in reference to Fascism; and *zipper*, a new invention, was trade-marked in 1925.

Of course, many new words of the 1920s are specifically linked to that decade: words like *Babbit* (a typical materialistic middle-class American of the time), *bootleg* (illicit liquor), *Charleston* (a popular dance of the era), *flapper* (a typically unconventional and frivolous young woman), *Lindy hop* (a dance named after the popular aviator Charles Lindbergh), *ritzy* (swanky, elegant, like the Ritz hotels), and the *Lost Generation* (the expatriate intellectuals of post–World War I). But even these words were not fly-by-night, but terms of genuine historical interest that are still in use.

What Dictionaries Show Us

The English language has today a larger vocabulary than most languages of the world. A comparison of the contents of English monolingual dictionaries since the 1700s suggests the extent of the expansion. One of the earliest modern English dictionaries, Samuel Johnson's *Dictionary of the English Language* (1755), contained about 50,000 entries. The next dictionary classic, Noah Webster's *American Dictionary of the English Language* (1828), included about 75,000 entries. The numbers kept increasing throughout the 1800s as dictionary makers strove to excel in their coverage of the English lexicon. The broadest coverage of English words occurred in the twentieth century. *Webster's Third New International Dictionary*, which appeared to great fanfare (and controversy) in 1961, claimed 450,000 entries. Almost fifty years later, the great *Oxford English Dictionary* lists approximately 616,500 word forms (free forms, combining forms, compounds, derivatives, phrases, etc.).

How Many Words Are in English?

There is little doubt that the English vocabulary has expanded greatly over the centuries. Compare the number of new words recorded in the five centuries between 1400 and 1900:

1400–1499:	1,025 words
1500–1599:	36,553 words
1600–1699:	48,232 words
1700–1899:	93,205 words

The difference in numbers between the 1400s and the 1800s is striking. One obvious reason for the huge discrepancy is that by the nineteenth century, more words were being collected by dictionary editors, like James Murray (1837–1915) of the *Oxford English Dictionary*, than ever before. Nevertheless, the size of the actual expansion is much in question. The lexicographer Sidney I. Landau, in *Dictionaries: The Art and Craft of Lexicography* (1984), presented the problem squarely: "How large is the English lexicon? Allen Walker Read [in *Current Trends in Linguistics*, vol. 10, 1972] estimates its extent at about four million. He adduces this figure by citing 700,000 words in the Merriam-Webster files [only a fraction of which make it into the dictionary] and at least one million words in the scientific vocabulary."

Landau goes on to disavow on many grounds Read's estimate. "The question, How many words are in the English language?" he writes, "cannot be answered in any satisfactory way. It depends on what one means by 'words' and by 'English', and even if one could decide the limits to each, the answer would be little more than a guess." Or, as Philip B. Gove, the editor of *Webster's Third,* puts it in his preface, "This dictionary has a vocabulary of over 450,000 words. . . . By itself, the number of entries is, however, not of first importance. The number of words available is always far in excess of . . . the number that can possibly be included."

Reasons for Growth

Although dictionaries are limited in their coverage, they do reflect the steady growth of our vocabulary. This growth has been due largely to the great expansion of the communications media during the last century and is itself a reflection of that expansion. Radio and television, the Internet, artificial satellites (there are now over twenty-four hundred orbiting the earth), the international press, and the current wireless smartphones—all communicate to the world instantly anything new, including every new coined word. And newly minted coinages proliferate (think *weblog, weblogger, blogger, blog, blogging, bloggerati, blogosphere, blogospherics, blogistics*), thanks to writers and speakers seeking new forms of expression and feeling free to make up words, to the extent that the line between the usage labels *formal, informal,* and *slang* is steadily blurring.

How New Words Are Formed

Where did the new words and meanings of the last century come from? Most were native coinages, words created by well-established processes like back-formation (*baby-sit* from *baby-sitter*), clipping or shortening (*condo* from *condominium, nuke* from *nuclear*), contraction (*helluva* from *hell of a*), blending (*smog* from *smoke* and *fog*), derivation (*televiewer, telecast, telegenic*), and compounding (*barfly, busywork*). A considerable percentage were borrowings from foreign languages (*garage, limousine, Lebensraum, daiquiri*).

These processes had been long at work in the language. Compounding, for example, was common in Old English, which abounded in compounds like *sweordbora* "swordbearer," *ealdormann* "alderman," and *grindetothum* "grind tooth" (i.e., molar). Old English also borrowed words from Latin and Greek, for example, *strēt* "street" (Latin *strata*), *disc* "dish" (Latin *discus*), *magester* "master" (Latin *magister*), *biscop* "bishop" (Greek *epískopos*), and *cirice* "church" (Greek *kūriakón*). As the use of these processes accelerated over the centuries, they became the basis of countless new words.

The Explosive Growth of New Words

The chapters that follow will list and discuss, decade by decade, the new words that have come into English in America since the year 1900. They provide an overview of the explosive growth of English during the past hundred-and-change years, and thereby cast a light, from a language standpoint, on the evolution of American culture. Before 1900 communication was slow and limited, and information could only be obtained by word of mouth, letter writing, and reading newspapers and books. There was no radio, and the telephone was in its infancy, as was the phonograph. All the modern means of communicating were still to come: motion pictures, television, computers, the Internet, cell phones. The electronic revolution made the transmission and popularization of new words inevitable. A famous hypothesis proposed by the American linguists Edward Sapir and Benjamin Lee Whorf is that the structure of a language influences and often shapes a people's culture. If we accept this hypothesis, we may surmise that not only has the expanding American culture influenced the growth of the English language, but also that American English has played a great part in shaping our culture.

The moment a new idea, concept, thought, or object is invented, someone in America is impelled to coin a word for it. Most of such coinages have a short life span, but many survive and attain longevity. Some words may go out of fashion but do not disappear from the language; they continue to exist as dated, dialectal, archaic, or obsolete words and are recorded as such in standard dictionaries. In short, the English language in America keeps growing and growing, like Topsy in *Uncle Tom's Cabin,* and for everything new in American English THERE'S A WORD FOR IT.

Chapter 1

The Dawn of the Twentieth Century:

1900–1909

L ife during the first decade of the 1900s was closer to the past than to the future. The great advances of the twentieth century were still to come. Consider these facts: the life span of an average American was about forty-seven years (nowadays it is seventy-eight). The weekly wages of an average worker in 1900 was about $10, and to earn that he had to work ten hours a day for six days of the week. Child labor was rampant. The city poor, many of them recent immigrants, lived in filth and were riddled with disease. Among city dwellers, food was scarce and sanitation almost nonexistent.

And yet people looked back at an even bleaker past and thought that things were looking up. After all, there were new inventions like the telephone and the automobile. Never mind that having a telephone in a house was a rare luxury or that cars were loud, smelly, and too fast (speed limits of twenty miles an hour were considered dangerous). It was progress. To the millions of immigrants huddled in masses in the big cities, America was the new promised land, the golden land of the future.

The term *melting pot* became a common metaphor for the process of assimilating the new immigrants in the United States into one great American culture. The term was popularized by the 1908 play *The Melting Pot*, by the English-born writer Israel Zangwill. In the play, which is set in New York City, the immigrant protagonist, David Quixano, declares: "Understand that America is God's Crucible, the great Melting-Pot where all the races of Europe are melting and reforming! A fig for your feuds and vendettas! Germans and Frenchmen, Irishmen and Englishmen, Jews and Russians—into the Crucible with you all! God is making the American." When the play opened in Washington, D.C., in 1909, President Theodore Roosevelt leaned over the edge of his box and shouted, "That's a great play, Mr. Zangwill, that's a great play!"

President Roosevelt, who was popularly known as "Teddy," also added a new word to the language, though not intentionally. During a hunting trip to Mississippi in 1902, Roosevelt's aides caught a black bear, tied it to a tree, and asked the president to shoot it. Roosevelt refused. The incident was depicted in a cartoon that showed a small and cute little bear being saved by the president. An enterprising businessman, inspired by the cartoon, created a toy in the form of a little stuffed bear cub and called it "Teddy's bear." Since then *teddy bears* have found their way into toy stores everywhere to the delight of little children.

Entertainment for children was limited mostly to toys and games in the early 1900s. As Dan Rather writes in *Our Times: America at the Birth of the Twentieth Century* (1996), "In his newspapers of January 1, 1900, the American found no such word as 'radio,' for that was yet twenty years from coming; nor 'movie,' for that, too, was

mainly in the future." The *nickelodeon*, a movie theater
with an admission fee of one nickel, was all the rage
because it was so affordable an entertainment. "There is
no town of any size in the United States which does not
contain at least one nickelodeon," reported the October
1908 issue of the *World To-day*.

The decade's newest and most surprising invention
was the *Escalator*, or "moveable stairway." The word
Escalator, which first appeared in 1900, was coined by
adding the ending *-ator* (in *elevator*) to the French-origin
word *escalade* (ultimately from Medieval Latin *scalare*
"to scale"). After its inventor sold the rights to the Escalator to the Otis Elevator Company, Otis failed to maintain
the word's status as a capitalized trade name, and in 1950
the U.S. Patent Office ruled that the lowercase word *escalator* had passed into public domain. Most people think
that *escalator* was formed from the verb *escalate*, but the
opposite is true. The verb *escalate* appeared in 1922 and
meant "to climb on an escalator." *Escalate* was a back-
formation from *escalator*, and it wasn't until about 1960
that it took on the meaning "to increase by degrees," as in
Prices are escalating. In turn, the noun *escalation* was
derived in 1938 from the verb.

Borrowing words from foreign languages was considered ultramodern and sophisticated at the century's turn.
French especially was regarded as the language of elegance par excellence; among the newest French loans
were *arriviste* (1901), a pushy or ambitious person, an
upstart, literally "one eager to arrive," first recorded in
a letter by Gabrille Gissing, wife of the late-Victorian

novelist George Gissing; *voyeur* (1900), one who derives pleasure from secretly observing others, a Peeping Tom, first found in an English translation of a French work on the sexual instinct; *déjà vu* (1903), the illusion of having experienced a present situation in the past, literally "already seen"; *cri de cœur* (1905), an anguished cry of distress, literally "a cry of (the) heart"; *haute couture* (1908), high fashion, literally "high dressmaking"; the interjection *touché* (1904), an exclamation used to indicate a hit in fencing, literally, "touched," which by 1907 was used figuratively to acknowledge a valid point or rejoinder made by someone.

It wasn't a coincidence that the French loanwords *garage* and *limousine* came in to English at the same time, in 1902. Carmakers, eager to make the automobile a status symbol, went to France to polish their terminology. There were no one- or two-car garages in 1902. The word *garage* referred to a building in which many cars were stored when not in use, something like today's parking garage. The word was considered foreign enough to put between single quotes or italicized in periodicals, as in the January 11, 1902, issue of the *London Daily Mail:* "The new 'garage' founded by Mr. Harrington Moore, hon. secretary of the Automobile Club . . . has accommodation for eighty cars." The French word was derived from the verb *garer* ("to shelter"). While the British, bowing to old tradition, promptly Anglicized the word, pronouncing it GAIR ij, the more style-conscious Americans made a point of pronouncing it ge RAZH in as close an approximation to the French pronunciation as they could. The early *lim-*

ousine was a large luxurious car with an enclosed compartment for the passengers and a separate compartment for the driver, originally without a roof. It was named after the French word for a protective cloak used by drivers when the car had no roof, and ultimately from *Limousin*, a region in central France (capital, *Limoges*). By the mid-1920s, these cars were so popular that they were familiarly referred to as limos.

German was another popular source of borrowings, especially of a literary type. The term *Götterdämmerung*, literally "Twilight of the gods," title of the last of Richard Wagner's four operas in *The Ring of the Nibelung* cycle, was adopted in English in 1909 in the figurative sense of "total destruction or downfall, as in a great final battle." The term was used to describe some of the devastating battles in World Wars I and II. Two other German loans that are still widely used are *Sprachgefühl* (1902), an instinctive feeling for language, first recorded in Greenough and Kittredge's *Worlds and Their Ways* (1902), literally "speech-feeling," and *Übermensch* (1902), a superman, popularized by George Bernard Shaw, as in the preface to his play *Major Barbara* (1907), where he writes: "It is assumed on the strength of the single word Superman (Übermensch), borrowed by me from Nietszche, that I look for the salvation of society to the despotism of a single Napoleonic Superman."

Another notable term of the decade coined by George Bernard Shaw was *Bardolatry*. G.B.S. coined it in 1901 in the preface to his iconoclastic *Three Plays for Puritans* (including *The Devil's Disciple, Caesar and*

Cleopatra, and *Captain Brassbound's Conversion*). Shaw made up *Bardolatry,* meaning worship or adoration of Shakespeare, by blending *Bard* (of Avon), a popular epithet for Shakespeare, with (id)*olatry*. The coinage was intended to disparage the attitude of nineteenth-century Romantic critics like Thomas de Quincey and Samuel Coleridge, who not merely admired Shakespeare's works but could find no fault in them—in short, they worshipped the Bard. Here's what Shaw wrote in the preface: "It was the age of gross ignorance of Shakespear [his spelling] and incapacity for his works that produced the indiscriminate eulogies with which we are familiar. . . . So much for Bardolatry!" In his subsequent writings, Shaw coined *Bardolater* for a worshipper of Shakespeare, and *Bardolatrous,* meaning "characterized by Bardolatry," as in this 1914 passage: ". . . the familiar plea of the Bardolatrous ignoramus, that Shakespear's coarseness was part of the manners of his time."

The longest word in English happened to turn up in 1900. It was formed by gluing suffixes or prefixes to base words. By this process, British politicians concocted the word *antidisestablishmentarianism,* meaning, seriously, "opposition to those who oppose the establishment of a state religion." This sesquipedalian monster was created by adding the simple prefix *anti-* to the term *disestablishmentarianism,* itself a mouthful, that was cooked up in the 1880s by adding the prefix *dis-* and the suffixes *-arian* and *-ism* to the word *establishment.* The creation of this 1900 Frankenword was enough to prevent coiners from such agglutinations for the next hundred years.

Among the words that made news early in the decade was the verb *hospitalize* ("to put in a hospital"). The word first appeared in print in 1901, though no doubt it had been widely used in common parlance for years. The *Oxford English Dictionary* (*OED*) points out that the word was "frequently commented on as an unhappy formation," which accounts for its absence in the press before 1901. Opposition to this verb was in line with criticism of such verbs as *finalize, deputize, jeopardize, theorize,* and *prioritize,* which in the nineteenth century were condemned by critics as "pretentious and unnecessary jargon." Another common term first recorded in 1901 is *grass roots.* It appeared in Rudyard Kipling's novel *Kim* (about an Irish orphan growing up in India), where it means "the basis, source, or origin of something," as in *the grass roots of evil.* The extended meaning "ordinary citizens, as opposed to the leaders or elite parts of society" shows up first in 1912, in *McClure's Magazine:* "From the Roosevelt standpoint, . . . it was a campaign from the 'grass roots up.'"

The coinage and spread of the title of respect *Ms.* (a blend of *Miss* and *Mrs.*) as the equivalent of the maritally neutral *Mr.* is usually attributed to the feminist movement of the 1970s. However, the *Oxford English Dictionary* traces the use of *Ms.* to 1901, when a writer in the Humeston, Iowa, newspaper *New Era* reported in the December 4 issue that "As a word to be used in place of 'Miss' or 'Mrs.', when the addresser is ignorant of the state of the person addressed, the *Sunday Republican* [a newspaper of Springfield, Mass.] suggests a word of which

'Ms.' is the abbreviation, with a pronunciation something like 'Mizz.'" The next time the word is mentioned was in 1949, in the linguist Mario Pei's book *The Story of Language*, where he credits feminists with the word's coinage. The fact is that *Ms.* is a much older word than we've been led to believe, preceding its use by women's lib by seventy years.

The word *bunk*, meaning "empty talk, nonsense, humbug," was introduced to the public in 1900 by the writer and journalist George Ade in his book *More Fables*. The automobile magnate Henry Ford, known for his acerbic tongue, used it in a sardonic article he published in 1916 in the *Chicago Tribune:* "History," wrote Ford, "is more or less bunk. It's tradition. We don't want tradition. We want to live in the present, and the only history that is worth a tinker's damn is the history that we make today." *Bunk* was a clipped form of the earlier *bunkum, buncombe,* after *Buncombe* County, North Carolina, whose representative in Congress made long, dull speeches to satisfy his constituents. *Bunk* was one of many clippings that were popularized at the turn of the century by newspaper and magazine writers (who were always in a hurry), among them *dorm* (dormitory), *gas* (gasoline), *hon* (honey), *coke* (cocaine), *Coke* (Coca-Cola), *steno* (stenographer), *plane* (airplane), and *El* (elevated train).

News reporters of the time began to take other liberties with words, as by forming blends like *smog* (1905, a blend of *smoke* and *fog*), *dramedy* (1905, a blend of *drama* and *comedy*), and *spork* (1909, a blend of spoon and fork), and unusual compounds like *pussyfoot* (1903, to move stealthily like a cat) and *muckraker* (1906, one who exposes corruption or scandal). The term *muckraker* was formed in allusion to the man in John Bunyan's *Pilgrim's Progress* who "can look no way but downward" as he rakes muck with his tool, and it was applied to writers of reform-minded articles about prison conditions, political corruption, child labor, and so on. Two famous muckrakers were Lincoln Steffens, whose book *The Shame of the Cities* (1904) exposed urban political corruption, and Upton Sinclair, whose book *The Jungle* (1906) revealed deplorable conditions in the meat-packing industry.

Another early innovation was the pronounceable abbreviation *POTUS* (1903, *President of the United States*). According to William Safire (in *Safire's Political Dictionary*, Oxford University Press, 2008), the *POTUS* (often spelled *Potus*) was married to the *FLOTUS* or *Flotus*, the *First Lady of the United States*. In later years these shorthand names inspired others: *Vpotus* (for the vice president, pronounce VEE-po-tus), *Slotus* (for the VP's wife, the *Second Lady of the United States*), and *Scotus* (for the *Supreme Court of the United States*).

Among other common words that made their debut early in the decade were:

Achilles' tendon [1900].

The tendon of the heel. It was so called from the mythological story that as a baby, Achilles was dipped by his mother in the river Styx to make him invulnerable, but because she held him by the heel, it was not dipped and therefore remained vulnerable. When we want to refer to someone's weak point, we say that it's his or her Achilles' heel.

ballyhoo [1901]. Extravagant advertising. Originally, a barker's spiel. According to the *OED*, the word was perhaps clipped from Irish English *ballyhooly*, used instead of "hell" to suggest chaos, confusion, and so on, from the name *Ballyhooly*, a village in County Cork, Ireland, "notorious for faction fighting." The verb *ballyhoo*, "to advertise extravagantly," appeared in 1911.

electrify [1900]. To supply (a factory, railroad, region, etc.) with electric power. The word was actually coined by Benjamin Franklin in 1727 in the sense of "to apply electric current to (a person)."

exurban [1901]. Belonging to a region beyond the suburbs. This word preceded by half a century the coinage of *exurbia* and *exurbs*, "the region beyond the suburbs inhabited by the well-to-do," both coined in the 1950s by A. C. Spectorsky and popularized in his book *The Exurbanites*.

Hall of Fame [1901]. A place where famous people are commemorated, such as the Baseball Hall of Fame at Cooperstown, New York. The name is first recorded in the magazine *The Land of Sunshine* (January 6, 1901), which refers to "The Columbia College 'Hall of Fame' [which] includes various more or less useful Americans and excludes Edgar Allan Poe."

hillbilly [1900]. A backwoods person, especially of the U.S. South. First described in the *New York Journal* (April 23, 1900) as "a free and untrammeled white citizen of Alabama, who lives in the hills, has no means to speak of, dresses as he can, talks as he pleases, drinks whiskey when he gets it, and fires off his revolver as the fancy takes him."

manic-depressive [1902]. A person suffering from bipolar disorder (periods of mania alternating with periods of depression). The adjective, as in *manic-depressive insanity*, appeared in 1901 as a translation of German *manisch-depressiv* in Emil Kraepelin's *Psychiatrie* (1899).

mannequin [1902]. A person employed to model clothes; a fashion model. The sense of a model or representation of a human figure for display of clothes first appeared in 1939. From French, from Dutch *manikin*, literally, "little man."

mutant [1901]. A term used in biology for any organism or form that has undergone mutation. Use of the term in science fiction for any abnormal or grotesque individual created by genetic mutation is first found in 1938 in E. Hamilton's *Weird Tales*.

pacifism [1902]. Opposition to war or violence, especially in international affairs. The term is first used at the 1902 Proceedings of the 10th Universal Peace Congress, after French *pacifisme* (1901).

ping-pong [1900]. The game of table tennis. The game's name took the country (and much of the world) by storm in the early years of the decade, to the point that it elbowed out a previous name, *table tennis* (1887). It was first spelled *Ping-Pong*, after the trade name for table tennis equipment; the name was coined in imitation of the sound made by the ball hitting the table.

pointillism [1901]. A painting technique using dots of pure color, developed by French neoimpressionists, especially Georges Seurat (1859–91). From French *pointillisme*, from *pointiller*, "to mark with points."

radiology [1900]. The branch of medicine dealing with radiation or X-rays. It was first used in the magazine *Popular Science Monthly* in the name "International Congress of Medical Electrology and Radiology."

Rosetta stone [1902]. Something that serves as a key to understanding some previously incomprehensible thing. A figurative use of the name given to a stone slab discovered in 1799 near Rosetta, a town in Egypt, bearing indecipherable inscriptions in Greek, demotic, and hieroglyphics (finally deciphered after 1822).

spoonerism [1900]. A transposition of the sounds of words, often with humorous results, as in "You're occupewing my pie" for "You're occupying my pew" and "The bean is dizzy" for "The dean is busy." Named after the English clergyman W. A. *Spooner* (1844–1930), who was noted for such involuntary tongue twisters.

Stetson hat [1900]. First found advertised in a 1900 catalogue, *American Mail Order Fashions.* Named after J. B. *Stetson* (1830–1906), who manufactured the broad-brimmed, high-crowned hat popular in the West.

A Selection of New Words of the 1900–1909 Decade

1900

Achilles' tendon, acidosis, anglophone, arbitrage (v.), art moderne, autopsy (v.), backup, bull (= bull's-eye), bunk (= humbug), calibrator, chesty, combinability, come-hither, Congolese, crawlsome, crescendo (v.), defeminize, dorm, effortful, egocentric, escalator, ethanol, expansionism, familial, fed up, frame-up, francophone, glob, goo-goo eyes, grizzly, gutful, Hall of Shame, hillbilly, illusional, Klondiking, low frequency, malariologist, mazuma, menarche, Mendel's law, misattribute (v.), Mongolism, mop-up, mot juste, motorcyclist, netball, nincompoopery, nonstop, peacherino, pedology, ping-pong, pint-sized, pole-vault (v.), preppy, radiology, rough-house (v.), side-step (v.), spoonerism, Stetson hat, summa cum laude, tendentious, voyeur, Zeppelin

1 9 0 1

aloofly, antibody, antiserum, arriviste, arty, backchat, ballyhoo, bardolatry, barrette, bionic, biota, birthing, bollix (v.), bulbosity, Caerphilly cheese, Capricornian, caption (v.), carnivory, centum, citrous, clop, communality, defreeze, dependability, devirilize, eatery, editorialist, exurban, eyeball (v.), fly-over, Gibson girl, googly, Hall of Fame, homocentric, hospitalize, huevos rancheros, hydroplane, ikebana, karat, la-di-da (v.), motorize, Ms., muralist, mutant, naturopathy, nim (game), noble gas, nonachiever, okapi, offbeat, overgraze, overintellectualize, peeve (v.), pinch-hitting, ping-pong (v.), pink slip, pizzeria, pointillism, power politics, press-agent (v.), racialist, reorder (n.), rev (= revolution), rewrite (n.), safety razor, satem, short-term (adj.), sizzler, tip-off, tippy-toe (v.), tractor, transocean (adj.), upstate

1902

airport, all clear, artsy-craftsy, arty-and-crafty, brisling, Brownie (camera), buttinsky, cartoonery, catalyst, cross-reference (v.), curvy, dancey, demographical, electronic, fado, foolproof, hookworm, junior varsity, looseleaf, made-to-order, manic-depressive, mannequin, mess-up, moo goo gai pan, motorboat, motorcycle (v.), neo-Marxist, nouveau art, oceanological, overstroke, overswing, pacifism, paranoid, photoreception, politicalization, racialism, Rhodes scholarship, Rosetta stone, sexology, squiggle, Sprachgefühl, subset, suitcase, teddy bear, towelette, trivia, Übermensch, windshield

1903

affenpinscher, artify, bar and grill, basically, blintze, bloc, bobskate, bohunk, buffalo (v.), Bundt (cake), Burberry (coat), Casanova, characterology, choo-choo, chug-a-lug, citywide, clone (n.), crosswise, déjà vu, doozy, dud (adj.), dybbuk, fandom, fink, flashback, founding (adj.), fountain (v.), fritto misto, garage, gerontology, headquarter (v.), high-powered, humidor, intimism, landfill, limousine, meunière (cookery), Middle Eastern, mishit (v.), moscato, motorbike, mudder, neuter (v.), New Art, nix (v.), optometrist, orthodontist, patsy, pediatrician, peekaboo (v.), POTUS, pussyfoot (v.), revisionism, Sherlock, short-change (v.), superman, throwaway, traumatize, vacuum cleaner

1904

accelerometer, amplitudinous, attaché case, back-track (v.), blouson, blue chip (poker), bombé, chiropractor, chromaticity, coaxial, corsetry, crude (oil), deactivate, desensitize, Deweyism, empathy, Everywoman, factionalism, Fraktur, freelance (v.), fuddy-duddy, geneticist, geo-politics, get-rich-quick, heartland, hypertensive, hypotensive, internist, junction (v.), Latinate, lallapaloosa, Luger, matrilineal (v.), off-Broadway, remainder (v.), remote control, Shavian, sideswipe (v.), ski (v.), speedometer, spotlight, suntan, tangelo, teletypewriter, touché, underpass, vamp, wisenheimer

1905

agelessness, ailurophobia, air speed, amaretto, anticoagulant, atmospherics, Biedermeier (period), bonhomous, bitsy, Browning (revolver), budo (martial arts), Christiania, Comstockery, controllability, cri de coeur, decompress, doodad, doyenne, drainboard, dramedy, end-product, euthenics, fungicidal, gas (= gasoline), haywire, helluva, hissy, hormone, humdinger, investigational, jolly (n.), kittenishness, Laika (dog), Lebensraum, luge, mahimahi (fish), metapsychic, minesweeper, muscle flexing, natto (dish), novocaine, operability, pad foot, parasympathetic, peg-leg (v.), penalty point, photomicroscopy, pinch hit, pin-spotter, play-by-play (adv.), player-piano, potsy, presto chango, production line, radiotherapist, Sinn Fein, skidoo (v.), sleuth (v.), smidge, smog, space-time, straphanger, teeter-totter, troubleshooter, twee, umpty, Victrola, Victorianism, yeah

1906

airplane, autosome, back-stabber, barfly, bromidic, butt-in, cannonball (v.), censorable, chemotherapy, chile ancho, coiffure (v.), concertina (v.), Cook's tour, cordless, counterterrorist, doll up, Dr Pepper, El (train), Everyman, freestyle, garage (v.), henna tattoo, hon (= honey), inactivate, industrialization, Inc., lotta, lowbrow, matrilocal, Menshevik, microfilm, minimalist, muckraking, Noilly Prat, Ovaltine, pacifist, Parker pen, patrilocal, pedophilia, pen-pushing, peptide, petit beurre, pillow book, pinscher, pop-up, powerboating, pushover, psychoanalysis, psychoanalytic, re-up, road test, shock absorber, sidekick, steno, sublet, subtotal, suffragette, talkfest, tightwad, tyrannosaurus, ultramicroscope, yup, zither (v.)

1907

activism, Adélie penguin, ampoule, anorexic, Ashcan school (of art), Bolshevik, changeover, charmeuse, chemotherapy, dopester, Dorothy bag, dyspraxia, egghead, élan vital, glom (v.), in-group, insightful, intelligentsia, krill, luftmensch, Meccano, Melba sauce, menopausal, Merry Widow, metastasize, mononucleosis, monoplane, moonscape, nosey parker, numerology, off-campus, one-shot, overprotective, Papillon (dog), parkland, planetology, preshrink (v.), publicize, punchy, radio- (combining form), Raffles, Romaine (lettuce), roustabout (v.), rubbery, sharecrop (v.), shock wave, snake and ladders, structuralism, syndicalism, taxi, taxicab, Tay-Sachs disease, television, Thermos, valorization

1908

additivity, addressograph, Africana, Afrikaans, airliner, antigen, bejesus, belay (n.), boob (= jail), caddy (v.), catatonic, chichi, chifforobe, coenzyme, co-host, coke (= cocaine), coupla, dammit, demi-vierge, dick (= detective), Dow-Jones, *E. coli*, electronics, expressionism, fatigability, filterable, genteelism, Grand Guignol, gunk, haute couture, insomniac, joy-ride, long-term, marginality, massivity, mudscape, nickelodeon, open-end, pacifistic, pep, Pernod, plane (= airplane), pooch (= dog), postwar, pretzel bender, prewar, ragtime (v.), razzle (v.), refinance (v.), rundown, semi-pro, social security, spermicide, stratosphere, take-out, verismo, whiz

1909

abstractionism, addict, A-frame, air-conditioner,
air-conditioning, air-cool (v.), attaboy, authoritarianism,
bipartisan, boomy, cagey, camp (adj. = effeminate), cinema,
clip-on, Coke (= Coca-Cola), conceptualize, counteroffensive,
desalt, dilly, downstate, downturn, elasticized, empathic,
force-feed, fuselage, futurism, gaffe, gallonage, gene,
geriatrics, Götterdämmerung, gun control, gyro, home-school
(adj.), hoopla, hickey, hydroplane (v.), immunology, instant
coffee, intermesh, jazz, judgmental, kewpie (doll), last-ditch,
libido, locational, maximalism, mediocrat, mind-set,
minimally, misandry, modernistic, mouth-to-mouth, movie,
musicology, mythomania, no-strings, orotundity,
orthodontics, oscilloscope, peeve (n.), peach Melba,
peoplehood, photoplay, playgroup, rabble-rousing,
scrounge (v.), show-me, smarmy, sorbent, sorption, speedball
(drug), spork, stickum, substandard, underemployment,
upcoast, upcurrent, up-to-the-minute, viewable,
Wassermann test, wish-fulfillment, workout, World War,
xenophobia

Chapter 2

The Ballroom Decade and the Great War:

1910–1919

The world was unprepared for the catastrophic war that engulfed it in the mid-1910s. The decade was known in the United States as the *Ballroom Decade*, with restaurants featuring dance floors where the *tango* and the *fox trot* were novel attractions. The tango was introduced in America in 1913 and was popularized by Rudolph Valentino in the silent film *The Four Horsemen of the Apocalypse*. The fox trot was a ballroom dance created in 1915 by Harry Fox, a vaudeville actor, and was originally referred to as "Fox's Trot." The *bunny hug* (1912) was another popular dance in ragtime rhythm. This was the decade when people took to the road in Ford's mass-produced *Model T* (also known as the *Tin Lizzie*) for its amazing speed of twenty-five to thirty miles per hour. In 1916, the *convertible* with its collapsible hood made its debut, and a year later *jaywalkers* began defying fast-moving taxis.

Mass entertainment consisted primarily of motion pictures, called since 1909 *movies* (short for *moving pictures*), but also called *films* (1911) and *cinema* (1909). Motion pictures without a soundtrack were known as *silent films* (1918), the *talkies* to appear three years later (1921). Another popular pastime was the *crossword puzzle,* which was invented by Arthur Wynne, a Liverpool journalist, and was first published (in a diamond-shaped form) in the *New York World* on December 21, 1913. In the fine arts, the *avant-garde* (1910) introduced new forms of *abstraction* (1915, nonrepresentational art), including *post-impressionism, Cubism,* and *vorticism* (machinelike abstractions).

The decade also saw the birth of *jazz,* a form of music based on ragtime that became the hallmark of American musical art during the twentieth century. The word *jazz* had a modest beginning as a slang term meaning "spirit, vigor, energy." It first surfaced in 1913 among sportswriters to describe the vigorous and spirited play of San Francisco baseball teams. In 1916, the word was applied to a type of blues-influenced ragtime music played by New Orleans bands known as jazz bands. (The word was variously spelled until 1919 as *jass, jas, jaz, jasz, jazz.*) As for the word's actual origin, there are several theories. Among the most popular ones is that *jazz* came from a West African word (such as Mandingo *jasi,* "be out of character") that was brought to America by slaves. Another theory connects the word with the American slang word *jasm,* meaning "spirit, energy," first attested in 1860 as a variant of the earlier *jism* (1842), of unknown origin. A third connects *jazz* with a vulgar French verb *jaser,* meaning to copulate, a notion reinforced by a 1918–19 navy slang noun use of *jazz* meaning copulation. The growing popularity of jazz music in the 1920s prompted F. Scott Fitzgerald to title his 1922 book of

short stories *Tales of the Jazz Age,* which gave the 1920s
the memorable name of the *Jazz Age.*

Science was making important advances during the
decade, injecting into English important scientific terms
such as the following:

allergy [1911]. An extreme sensitivity to certain foods, pollens,
and other substances resulting in skin rash, sneezing or wheezing,
and so on. The term was borrowed from German *Allergie,* coined
in 1906 by an Austrian pediatrician, Clemens von Pirquet, from
Greek *állos* "other" + *érgon* "activity" + *-ia* "-y". Derived terms
are *allergic* (1911), *allergen* (1912, a substance inducing an
allergy), *allergenic* (1913), and *allergist* (1934, a physician special-
izing in the treatment of allergies).

Alzheimer's disease [1912]. A form of dementia marked by
progressive memory loss and mental deterioration. It was named
after Alois *Alzheimer,* a German neurologist, who described the
disease in 1907. He called it "presenile dementia," but his co-
discoverer of the disease, the German psychiatrist Emil Kraepelin,
named it after Alzheimer. The disease is sometimes mistakenly
called *Old-Timer's disease.*

autism [1912]. A developmental disorder characterized by
extreme self-absorption and detachment from reality. The term
was derived by the Swiss psychiatrist Eugen Bleuler from New
Latin *autismus,* formed from Greek *aùtós* "self" + *-ismus* "-ism."
Bleuler also coined the adjective *autistic* to designate the form of
thinking and behavior typical of autism.

chemotherapy [1910]. The treatment of disease, especially cancer, by means of chemicals. The term was borrowed from German *Chemotherapie,* coined in 1907 by the German bacteriologist Paul Ehrlich from the combining forms *Chemo-* + *Therapie* "therapy." The informal clipped form *chemo* is first recorded in the 1970s.

gene [1911]. The basic unit of heredity. The term was borrowed from German *Gen,* coined in 1909 by Wilhem Johannsen, a Danish botanist and geneticist, from Greek *-genēs* "born, produced." Johannsen also coined in 1909 the term *Genotypus,* borrowed in 1911 as *genotype,* "the genetic makeup of an organism." The terms *genetic* and *genetics* appeared in English earlier, in the 1800s.

moron [1910]. A mentally retarded person with an IQ of 50 to 69, according to a 1910 classification by the American Association for the Study of the Feeble-Minded. After the American humorist Robert C. Benchley generalized the word in 1917 in *Vanity Fair* to mean a very stupid or unintelligent person, an idiot, this meaning became widespread, and psychologists stopped using it in the original technical sense. The word was borrowed from Greek *mōrón,* neuter of *mōrós* "stupid."

vitamin [1912]. Any of the organic substances essential in small amounts to normal metabolism. It was coined as *vitamine* by Casimir Funk, a Polish American biochemist, from Latin *vīta* "life" + *amine,* from his mistaken idea that the substances were amines.

An unusual, semiscientific term that popped up, seemingly out of nowhere, early in the decade was *triskaidekaphobia,* meaning the fear of the number 13. The term's first appearance was in an article in 1911 by the American psychologist Isador H. Coriat, who coined it from the Greek words *treiskaideka* "thirteen" + *phobia* "fear." Fear of the number 13 is a superstition found in ancient times; for example, the Code of Hammurabi omits 13 in its list of numbers. A popular extension of the phobia is fear of Friday the 13th, given the name *paraskevidekatriaphobia* in the 1990s by the psychiatrist Donald E. Dossey. This fear seems also to be unfounded, though theories of its provenance abound. In the novel and film *The Da Vinci Code,* for example, the superstition is traced to the arrest of the Knights Templar on Friday 13, 1307. In Jewish and Christian tradition, however, the number 13 is not unlucky, as seen in the 13 attributes of God's mercy enumerated in the Book of Exodus. And boys who become bar mitzvahed and get tons of gifts when they turn 13 consider the number 13 a very lucky number indeed.

No one had anticipated a world war. The term *world war* was casually used once in 1909, but not until 1914 was *World War* applied to what was also called the *Great War,* a name originally used for the Napoleonic Wars (1803–1815). The Great War began with hostilities between Austria-Hungary and Serbia, but ultimately involved most of the nations of the world. The vocabulary of war flooded the last half of the decade: *air raid, ammo* (short for *ammunition*), *anti-aircraft, D-day* (code name for a day set to begin a military operation), *dogtag* (military identification tag), *fly-past* (aircraft procession), *foxhole, leatherneck* (a marine), *machine-gunner, strafe* (to attack with low-flying aircraft), *P.O.W. (prisoner of war)*. Toxic gas was first used on a large scale, producing in 1914–15 dreadful terms like *mustard gas, asphyxiating gas,* and *poison gas,* which produced *gas gangrene* and against which *gas masks* were used. Nicknames, mostly derogatory, for the German enemy became a psychological weapon and included *Boche* (from French), *Fritz, Kraut* (from German *Kraut,* "cabbage, vegetable"), and *Jerry* (clipped from *German*). Among the new weapons used in World War I was the *Bangalore torpedo* (introduced by a Royal engineer in Bangalore, South India), the *flamethrower* (translated from German *Flammenwerfer*), the *trench mortar* (a small mortar used in trench warfare), *camouflage* (from French), and the *depth charge* (a waterproof bomb to attack the German *U-boats,* from German *U-boot,* short for *Unterseeboot* "undersea boat").

The word *S.O.S.,* meaning an urgent call for help, took on special importance during the war. It was widely used as a signal in an emergency, though its users rarely knew what the letters stood for. The word was not an abbreviation. It first appeared in 1910 as an international radiotelegraphic signal of distress used especially by ships, consisting of the letters *S, O,* and *S* spelled out in Morse code, the letters having been chosen because they were easily transmitted in code. The word was so popular that by 1918 it was commonly used as if it were an abbreviation of various phrases, such as "same old story," "same old stuff," "same old slush" (referring to food).

The war also familiarized everyone with the word *sabotage,* borrowed from French in 1910. The word was defined in Edward S. Farrow's *A Dictionary of Military Terms* (1918) as "wanton destruction of property to embarrass or injure an enemy, such as the smashing of machinery, flooding of mines, burning of wheat and grain, destroying fruit and provisions, dynamiting reservoirs and aqueducts, tying up railroads, etc." The French word derived from the verb *saboter,* "to botch, destroy willfuly," originally "to make noise by striking shoes together," from *sabot* "shoe." *Sabotage* was also used as a verb by 1918, and one who committed sabotage was called by another French word, *saboteur.*

The United States stayed out of the war until 1917, so for many Americans the early 1910s were relatively peaceful years, with advances made in various fields, such as art and entertainment, sports, and science and technology. Some new terms of the period were *aerobatics* (feats of aviation), *backpack, decathlon, jai-alai* (the game of pelota), *movie star, pocket billiards, Technicolor, collage, surrealist, cellophane, margarine, phenobarbital, self-service, spritz, quantum theory, rickettsia, technocracy, white-collar,* and a heap of terms based on sex, including *sexy* (1912), meaning "sexually attractive," *sex object* (1911), *sex symbol* (1911), *sex appeal* (1913), and *sex drive* (1916).

Much of the interest in (and some might say, obsession with) sex was due to the growing influence of Sigmund Freud and his psychoanalytical theories. Anything having to do with Freud's theories was called *Freudian* (1910), such as the *Freudian slip,* an inadvertent mistake that supposedly reveals an unconscious motive or wish. Some of the Freudian terminology of the decade included the *Oedipus complex* (1910), "subconscious sexual feelings of a son toward his mother"; the *Electra complex* (1913), "subconscious sexual feelings of a daughter toward her father"; *the libido* (1909); *the unconscious* (1912); *fixation* (1910); and *repression* (1909). A new discipline, *sexology,* the systematic study of sexuality, was introduced in 1912 as a translation of the German *Sexualwissenschaft* ("sexual science"). The psychoanalytical theories of the Swiss psychiatrist Carl Gustav Jung also contributed influential *Jungian* terms during the decade, such as *psyche* (1910), "the total psychological apparatus of the mind"; *persona* (1917), "the outer aspect of a person's character"; and the contrasting characters of *extrovert* and *introvert* (1918).

Freud and Jung aside, the decade of the 1910s popularized certain other proper names, including:

Binet-Simon [1910]. An intelligence test for children, devised in 1905 by Alfred *Binet* (1857–1911) and Théodore *Simon* (1873–1961), French psychologists.

Bloomsbury [1914]. A literary, artistic, and intellectual center flourishing in the early twentieth century in England. From the name of a district in central London, north of the Thames River.

Borsalino [1914]. A man's wide-brimmed felt hat. Named after the Italian maker.

Chardonnay [1911]. A dry white wine. From the French name of the grape used in producing the wine.

Montessori [1912]. An educational method designed to teach young children to learn by doing things themselves. Named after Maria *Montessori* (1870–1952), who devised the method.

Pulitzer [1917]. An annual prize awarded in the United States for distinguished achievement in journalism, literature, drama, and music, established by Joseph *Pulitzer* (1847–1911), an American newspaper publisher.

Ritz [1910]. Any large, elegant hotel. From the name of the sumptuous hotels founded by the Swiss-born hotelier César *Ritz* (1850–1918). The adjective *ritzy* ("elegant, swanky") was derived from the proper name.

Savonarola [1916]. A fiercely puritanical person, especially in politics, religion, and the arts. Named after Girolamo *Savonarola* (1452–98), a Dominican friar during the Italian Renaissance who fiercely opposed the moral and political corruption of the clergy.

Svengali [1914]. A person who exerts a controlling or hypnotic influence on another, usually with evil intent. Named after *Svengali*, a fictional character in the novel *Trilby* (1894) by George Du Maurier, who hypnotizes the novel's tone-deaf heroine, Trilby, into becoming a great singer, with disastrous results when she emerges from her trance.

The language was gradually divesting itself of Victorian stuffiness and becoming increasingly informal, even slangy. Colloquial contractions like *gonna* (for *going to*), *kinda* (for *kind of*), and *woulda* (for *would have*) began to appear in print, as well as dialectal contractions like *y'all* (for *you-all*), as in "How're y'all this mornin'?" The suffix *-ee*, originally used in law to designate the beneficiary of an act (as in *payee, vendee, lessee, indorsee*), was now used loosely to denote the object of any act specified by a verb, as in *amputee, parolee, internee.* The old suffix *-eer*, denoting one who deals or works with something (as in *auctioneer, engineer, mountaineer*), turned derogatory, as in *patrioteer,* "one who pretends to be a patriot," and *profiteer,* "one who makes excessive or unfair profit," a usage leading in the 1920s to *racketeer.*

Shortly after the United States declared war against Germany, in April of 1917, George M. Cohan wrote the song that gave the name *Over There* to America's involvement in the war:

> *Over there, Over there,*
> *Send the word, send the word over there—*
> *That the Yanks are coming, The Yanks are coming*
> *The drums rum-tumming*
> *Everywhere.*
> *So prepare, say a pray'r,*
> *Send the word, send the word to beware.*
> *We'll be over, we're coming over,*
> *And we won't come back till it's over*
> *Over there.*

On November 11, 1918, an armistice was signed between the Allies and Germany, and World War I was at last over

"over there." November 11 was proclaimed *Armistice Day* in the United States, and in Canada it was named *Remembrance Day*. (In 1954, the U.S. Congress changed the name to *Veterans Day* to honor U.S. veterans of all the wars.) A peace treaty, known as the Treaty of Versailles, officially concluded the war. One of the articles of the treaty called for the formation of a *League of Nations* to settle future disputes between member countries through negotiation and diplomacy.

At the start of the next decade, the postwar spirit of optimism prevailed. In the wake of the war, a period of artistic and social renaissance took over America. It was the time of the Jazz Age and the Flapper Era.

A Selection of New Words of the 1910–1919 Decade

1910

age-old, amputee, avant-garde, beaver (= beard), Bildungsroman, brain trust, buntal (hat straw), busywork, cantilevered, chain store, cheerio (interj.), chemotherapy, cold-cream (v.), commercialese, commish (= commission), cooch (dance), cripes (interj.), curie, filterability, fixation, Freudian, gink (= fellow), go (adj. = ready), grabby (adj.), harisa (dish), immunology, jai alai, keystroke, kitchenette, klaxon, Lincolnesque, mixed grill, moron, night letter, nuts (interj.), Oedipus complex, pantywaist, phoniness, photodrama, photoplay, pinch runner, pipe-dream (v.), pipsqueak, plottage, post-impressionism, prankster, psyche, psychoanalyst, pussyfoot (adj.), quarterbacking, rummy (card game), rustproof, sabotage, scrapie, slype (basketry), small-time, Strega (liqueur), sunbake (v.), taramasalata, twofer, tutu, underfoot, undernourished

1911

Air Force, airmail, allergic, allergy, battle cruiser, brassière, bratwurst, claustrophobe, coo (interj.), Cubism, desex (v.), floozy, gene, genotype, get-together, hatha-yoga, hi (= high), higher-up, hoosegow, hophead, ivory tower, jinx (n.), lettergram, make-work, manic depression, misdiagnose, mislabel, motion study, mothercraft, mozzarella, no-hitter, offpeak, outdoorsy, out-of-towner, part-timer, pen-pusher, photocopier, pickoff, pie in the sky, pinch-hit (v.), poison pen, polio, poop (= information), pronto, psychoanalyze, Rotarian, right-on, scatty, self-cleansing, Sen-Sen, sex object, sex symbol, taupe, taxi (v.), Tortoni, underinsure, vamp, Waldorf salad, wienie, X-chromosome, Y-chromosome, zing (n.)

1912

Alzheimer's disease, affectless, ambivalence, autism, autistic, blues, Buddhology, boner, bunny-hug, cellophane, chef (v.), coverage, decathlon, deviate (n.), dupe (v. = duplicate), frumpiness, gangland, germy, gorm, highball (v.),

hometown, Imagism (movement in poetry), Imagist,
long-playing, immunologist, irregardless, Jack (cheese),
kinda, low-rent, lunker, masculinist, nosedive (n.),
overprivileged, packsaddle (v.), pep, percentagewise, pie-
faced, Piltdown, profiteer, pulchritudinous, punch-drunk,
quantum theory, rinky-dink, Rolex, sand-yacht,
schizophrenia, sex-linked, sexology, sexy, songfest,
steam-roller (v.), tweedy, verboten, vernissage, vigorish,
vitamin, yesman

1913

amnesiac, antifreeze, balibuntal, behaviorism, blackout,
body-surfing, celeb, child-free, clientelism, close-up,
crossword puzzle, Electra complex, fifty-fifty, followership,
free line (fishing), geneticist, girl power, gonna, grandkid,
groceteria, histamine, home-wrecker, illegit, info, jargoneer,
koine, lead-in, manpower (v.), marathoning, mincy,
motorbiking, motorcade, movie house, movie star, nada,
Neanderthaler, Nebuchadnezzar (bottle), neo-orthodoxy,
nickel-and-dime (v.), not-for-profit, off-flavor, once-over,
ozeki (sumo), Pentecostalist, pep talk, person-to-person,
pot-shot (v.), pull-on (adj.), rotogravure, Rubenesque,
seaplane, sex appeal, shillaber (= decoy), shopping list,
spic, stooge, swank, swizzle, turnaround, vaudevillian,
whoop-up, woulda, yessir, zero (v.), Ziegfeld, zowie

1914

air raid, anesthesiology, antivirus, aquaplane, asthenosphere, backpack, billiken (mascot figure), bing (interj.), birth control, blurb, Boche, countable, devaluation, dog-and-pony show, doohickey, endocrine, ephedra, eroticize, feeb, filmization, filmize, film star, fly-past, folky, fuddydud, functionalism, functionalist, Georgianism (Georgian style), gesundheit, gunsel, headphone, heel (= bad person), hypersensitivity, Indianapolis 500, insulin, jake (= O.K.), laissez-passer, leatherneck, legalese, malihini, mandocello, milonga, monetarist, Mountie, movieland, multiple-choice, newsreel, nitwit, olé, podiatry, preatomic, rabbit punch, Realpolitik, retread, shish kebab, stash (cache), Svengali, troposphere, vorticism

1915

abstraction (art), adland, aerobatics, airbrush (v.), America First, anadama bread, back-to-nature, bomber, conurbation, Croix de Guerre, cushy, debus (v.), Dobos torte, (all of a) doodah, downer, downwash, embus (v.), frosh, futuristic, gassed, gelation, grifter, homeroom, kakotopia, killing field, Kodachrome, machine-gunner, narcissistic, nightscape, nosedive (v.), parolee, playlist, pogrom (v.), posh (adj.), possibilism, press officer, pressure cooker, puppeteer, rabbit punch, radio frequency, schlock, shiv, smoke screen, soft-pedal (v.), strafe (v., n.), ump, wino, yo-yo

---

1916

ambivalent, biome, Blimp, Brillo, Bromo, carcinogenic, counterattack (v.), cryptobiotic, cuckoo-land, dagnab it, dealership, dupe (= duplicate film), dysfunction, echt, economy size, ecotype, environmentalist, excludable, glottalize, goof (n.), grouch (v.), homo-erotic, hush-hush, jarhead, looey, low-maintenance, Machtpolitik, Midwesterner, Mitteleuropa, moviedom, multimillion, munitioneer, national service, one-nighter, op (= operation), over the top, pastrami, Pelmanism (memory training), penny-pincher, photofinishing, photonovel, primatologist, princessy, profiteer (v.), prosit (interj.), Proto-Indo-European, punchline, Realtor, recirculate, R.O.T.C., Schick test (anti-diphtheria), seral, sex drive, shill (n.), shrewdie, steel helmet, well-scrubbed, time-space, trip-wire

---

1917

airdrome, ammo, Arian, ashram, Aussie, ball hawk, blotto, Bolshevism, Bolshevist, boogie, camouflage (n., v.), careerist, catwalk, chauffeur (v.), chowhound, chucklesome, conchy (n.), conk (v.), cootie, Doberman pinscher, duckboard, earful, egg foo yung, emote (v.), enlistee, filthy (v.), gah (interj.),

gel (v.), G-man, goofus, grunion, hokum, jaywalker, jazzbo,
jazz up, Leninist, lookit, machinable, machine-gun (v.),
marlin, mopper-up, moronic, munchie, Mutt and Jeff,
narcissist, nosher, obscurist, package (v.), part-work, pep pill,
persona, pinpoint (v.), Pollyanna, psych (v.), racialist, Red
Guard, Soviet, sideswipe, soft-focus, spritz (v.), stainless steel,
stateship, storm-troops, sub-deb, tailspin, takeover,
Technicolor, trade-in, windup

1918

baby blues, blah, Bolshie, breakthrough, buck private,
choccy, congresswoman, culturalization, D-day, decertify,
defeatism, defeatist, devalue, Europocentric, extrovert,
fadeout, farmerette, force-feed (n.), Girl Guiding, grouse
(n.), humanoid, hush-puppy, imbecilic, Indianization,
ineducability, internee, intragroup, in-transit, introvert,
Leninism, mag (= magneto), major (v.), majoritarian,
maladapted, marionettist, mech (= mechanic), Mickey Finn,
mixability, motorboating, multistory, Murphy bed, narcissistic,
neo-Marxism, neo-nationalist, nifty (n.), Okie, oo-la-la,
patootie, patrioteer, pigeoneer, pip (v.), pitch-in dinner,
politicization, poster (v.), Potemkin village, pre-med,
recon, Red Army, roomie, rurban, rustproofing, scrimpy,
shimmy (n.), speedster, streamline (v.), surrealist, umpteen,
zoom (n.)

1919

ad-lib (v.), air freight, aircraft carrier, airmail (v.), aliyah,
barbital, bimbo, child-minding, collage, comb-out, copacetic,
co-star (v.), criminogenic, cross-selling, culturalism,
decontrol, delouse, dunk (v.), encirclement, encode, foxhole,
heavy-lift, high-profile, hippy (= large-hipped), incendivity,
jazzy, mercurochrome, mandated, middleness, motor scooter,
mud-sling (n.), mush (v.), musicalize, Naugahyde,
noodlehead, offline, one-world (adj.), oompah (v.), ovenette,
overreact, parliamentarization, payables, payphone, penne,
permanentize, phenobarbital, phooey, pissoir, pokey, posh (v.),
precast (v.), presoak (n.), press officer, put-on, putsch, radio
(v.), red ink, red-light (v.), reorg, rickettsia, sado-masochism,
safety-pin (v.), self-service, semi-trailer, shimmy (v.), skyway,
snooty, supersonic, synergize, synchronized, technocracy,
Trotskyite, tweenie, walk-up, white-collar, wonky, yawl
(= y'all), zing (v.)

Chapter 3

The Roaring Twenties:

1920–1929

The 1920s have been called by many names: the *Jazz Age,* the *Roaring Twenties,* the *Booming Twenties,* the *Flapper Era,* all alluding to the carefree, lighthearted, ebullient spirit of the times following the depressing years of the First World War. The slangy vocabulary of the early 1920s reflected that spirit: *the bee's knees, the cat's meow, the cat's pajamas*—all meaning "the best, the greatest, the most wonderful." Instead of "ladies and gentlemen," *boys and girls* became an informal form of address. New slangy or informal usages included *delish* for "delicious," *gaga* for "silly, crazy" (from French), *nah* for "no," and *wow* for "a great success, a hit." In 1922, the critic and satirist H. L. Mencken coined and popularized the term *booboisie* "stupid people (boobs) as a class," blending *boob* and *bourgeoisie,* and in the same year *nobrow* (less brainy than a *lowbrow*) appeared. And in 1923, the disparaging name *Babbitt* (after the main character of Sinclair Lewis's 1922 novel of the same name) was used to denote a materialistic and complacent middle-class American of the time.

Though a *flapper* meant a typically unconventional and frivolous young woman of the '20s, the term had a prehistory dating back to the slang of the 1890s. In James

Redding Ware's *Passing English of the Victorian Era* (1909), *flapper* is defined as "a very immoral young girl in her early 'teens'." According to the *OED*, the term is commonly supposed to be a figurative use of an earlier meaning (1747) of the word, "a young wild duck or partridge." It was popularly believed in the 1920s that F. Scott Fitzgerald had created the image of the flapper in his stories, but he disavowed the notion in an interview for *Metropolitan Magazine*. "I had no idea of originating an American flapper when I first began to write," he said. "I simply took girls whom I knew very well and, because they interested me as unique human beings, I used them for my heroines."

It was the title of a silent movie released in 1927 about a shopgirl in love with the heir of the largest store in the world. Clara Bow played the part of the shopgirl, and so the actress came to be known as the *It girl*. The story centers on the problems our heroine faces due to her low birth; but she possesses "it"—a quality described in the film as that "which draws all others with its magnetic force." The epithet has since been used for any young woman with great sex appeal, as in this from the *New York Times* of August 17, 2008: "Overnight, Ms. Zhukova's new center and her . . . billionaire, art-collecting boyfriend, have made her an art-world It Girl."

The times were ripe for the cultivation of feminine beauty. A galaxy of beauty specialists known as *beauticians* descended on American cities, opening *beauty parlors* and *beauty salons*, where with a liberal application of cosmetics they transformed frumpy housewives into ravishing Galateas. Beauty pageants had been around since the turn of the century, but the first modern beauty contest, featuring *bathing beauties,* took place in 1921 in Atlantic City. A Miss Margaret Gorman of Washington won the contest and was named *beauty queen,* earning the title of "Miss America," after which the contest became known as the *Miss America Pageant.* A less socially acceptable exposure of the body, imported from Germany, was communal *nudism.* Its practitioners called themselves *nudists,* though to emphasize that theirs was a natural way of life, they often chose to call themselves *naturists.*

Good times meant good eating, and *haute cuisine,* or high-class cooking, attracted many Americans—but not just to French cuisine. The bon vivants of the 1920s dined not only on *fettuccine Alfredo* (named after restaurateur Alfredo Di Lelio), *chicken Tetrazzini* (named after the Italian soprano Luisa Tetrazzini), or Mexican *guacamole* (from Nahuatl *ahuacamolli,* "avocado sauce"), but also savored exotic Japanese dishes like beef or chicken *sukiyaki* and deep-fried *tempura.*

The 1920s were a time when the new word *teenage* still sounded strange to the ears and appeared in print between quote marks (as in *"teenage" girls*); when *hitch-hiking* was always done by two or three "young Janes" hiking through one of the states; when battered old cars were called *jalopies* (so strange a word that in 1929 it was spelled *Jaloppi* and in 1936 *gillopy*); when *T-shirts* and *zippers* were new fashion items; and when calling an outstanding actor or performer "a star" was no longer regarded as sufficient—a word was needed for one who surpassed mere stardom. The novelist Warwick Deeping, in his novel *Sorrell and Son* (1925), came up with the word. It was *superstar*. Deeping's coinage was probably influenced by *superman*, George Bernard Shaw's English rendering of German *Übermensch* (coined by Nietzsche) in his 1903 play *Man and Superman*.

The flippant, fun-loving spirit of the Flapper Era was at times overshadowed by serious social issues that affected deeply the lives of many Americans. On January 29, 1920, the Eighteenth Amendment to the U.S. Constitution went into effect, inaugurating the era of national *Prohibition*, which was to last thirteen years. The amendment, which declared that "the manufacture, sale, or transportation of intoxicating liquors . . . is hereby prohibited," was the outcome of a long struggle between the *drys*, who supported Prohibition ("the Noble Experiment"), and the *wets*, who fought against it. Prohibition was also known as *Volsteadism*, after Andrew J. Volstead, the American lawmaker responsible for the Volstead Act, which established national Prohibition. Life during Prohibition made commonplace such terms as *speakeasy*, "a shop or bar where alcoholic drinks are sold illegally"; *bathtub gin*, "homemade gin made in a bathtub"; *bootleg*, "illicit liquor, so called because a bottle could be concealed in a tall boot"; *rumrunner*, "a trader in illicit liquor"; and *G-man*, redefined as "a Government agent who pursued rumrunners and smashed illegal stills."

A temperance activist named Delcevare King, of Quincy, Massachusetts, launched in 1923 a contest in which he offered $200 for a word that would characterize a person who broke the law by drinking illegally made or obtained liquor. On January 15, 1924, King announced the winning word. It was *scofflaw*, submitted by two contestants (who split the winnings) and chosen from more than twenty-five thousand other words sent in from all the states of the United States In 1936, H. L. Mencken, in the fourth edition of *The American Language*, wrote that *scofflaw* "came into immediate currency, and survived until the collapse of Prohibition." What Mencken, who died in 1956, did not foresee was that *scofflaw* would survive into the next century, albeit with the modified and more general definition of "one who flouts the law, especially by not paying fines he owes," as in this *New York Times* headline of April 17, 2008: "Iraq cracks down on seat belt scofflaws."

In postwar politics, supporters of *isolationism* ("advocacy of political isolation") opposed the League of Nations and won a resounding victory in the presidential election of 1920. Not everyone cheered at the election of an isolationist Republican, Warren G. Harding, especially war veterans who felt abandoned by their country. The generation of young people who lived through the "Great War" were known as the *Lost Generation*, a name popularized by Ernest Hemingway in his celebrated novel *The Sun Also Rises* (1926) with the epigraph "You are all a lost generation" on the title page. The name was also used for the expatriate artists and intellectuals who spent the postwar years in Europe, among them Hemingway himself.

During the 1920 presidential campaign, Warren Harding used the word *normalcy* in a torrent of alliteration promising a return to peace and stability: "America's present need is not heroics but healing, not nostrums but normalcy, not revolution but restoration, not agitation but adjustment, not surgery but serenity, not the dramatic but the dispassionate, not experiment but equipoise, not submergence in internationality but sustainment in triumphant nationality."

Harding's opponents could have easily ridiculed his excessive and unsubtle alliteration; instead, they seized upon the uncommon word *normalcy*, deriding it as a ridiculous malapropism, and insisting that the correct word was *normality*, since nouns with the suffix *-cy* derived from words ending in *-te* (as *intimacy* from *intimate*). Even though Harding won the 1920 election, he had to endure criticism throughout his tenure for his "misuse" of the word. However, his use of *normalcy* has long since been justified, mainly on the grounds that he did not invent the word, as was claimed by his critics, but found it in a dictionary.

In the world of art and literature, the word *Dada* and its derivatives *Dadaism* and *Dadaist(ic)* burst upon the English-speaking scene in 1920 as the most influential cultural movement of the age. The movement rejected traditional standards and conventions in art and literature with its *anti-art* message. The term *Dada* was borrowed from French, in which it was apparently coined from *être sur son dada* ("ride one's hobby horse"), the title of an article published in Zurich by Tristan Tzara (1896–1963), a Romanian artist and one of the founders of the movement. The famous French artist Marcel Duchamp

(1887–1968) was notoriously connected with Dada when
he submitted a urinal, which he titled "Fountain," to an
exhibit by the Society of Independent Artists, of which
Duchamp was a board member. The committee oversee-
ing the exhibit promptly rejected "Fountain" as not being
art, infuriating the Dadaists and causing Duchamp to
resign from the board.

Freudian psychology was making headway during
the 1920s. Three basic Freudian terms, *id, ego, superego,*
were made prominent by Freud in "Das Ich und das Es"
(literally, "The I and the It"), a paper published in 1923
and translated by Joan Riviere in 1924 as "The Ego and
the Id." The terms the *id,* the *ego,* and the *superego* were
translations of German *das Es, das Ich,* and *das Über-Ich,*
literally, "the It," "the I," and the "Over-I," which to
German readers were self-explanatory. Freud's translator,
however, sought the then more widely recognized Latin
words to convey his concepts.

A new school of psychology emerged in 1922, known
as *Gestalt psychology,* which held that mental or behavioral processes cannot be explained by analysis of their
component parts (as reflexes, reactions, sensations, etc.)
but must be studied as wholes or *Gestalts* (from German
Gestalt, "form, shape, configuration"). Gestalt psychology
was also called *Gestaltism,* and its adherents were known
as *Gestaltists.*

Among the scientific advances of the decade were
the discoveries of the hormone *estrogen,* the antibiotic
penicillin, the subatomic particle *proton,* the quantum
of light *photon,* and the astronomical *cosmic rays.* The

accomplishments of science inspired a brand-new genre of creative writing, *science fiction*, typical of which was the invention of the *robot*. A futuristic term, *robot* appeared in English in 1923, two years after the premiere of the play *R.U.R.* (for *Rossum's Universal Robots*) by the Czech playwright Karel Čapek (1890–1938). The play is a fantasy, dealing with manlike machines called *robots* created for slave labor in Rossum's factory. After a scientist endows them with emotions, the robots revolt against their masters and take over the world. The word *robot* derives from Czech *robota* "hard work, drudgery" and is related to German *Arbeit* "work." Out of science fiction came real science, the production of programmable automatons that perform a multiplicity of tasks. *Robotics*, "the science and technology of robots," was coined in 1941 by the science fiction writer Isaac Asimov, but has since been used to mean "the use of robots in industrial automation."

In Europe, the 1920s were marked by the emergence of the *Fascisti*, a group of Italian nationalists formed in 1919 to fight communism. Led by Benito Mussolini, the *Fascists* (also known as the *Blackshirts* from the color of their uniform shirts) influenced the creation of other authoritarian right-wing groups in Germany, Hungary, Romania, and other countries, all of which came to be known as Fascists. The Fascists called their heads "the leader"; thus, Mussolini was called *Il Duce* (or *the Duce*) and Hitler *der Führer* (or *the Führer*).

In America, though, the decade heralded progress. A milestone in education was achieved with the development of the *intelligence quotient,* or *IQ,* to measure the degree of a person's intelligence in relation to the average for the age group, which is fixed at 100. Around the same time, the term *New Negro* appeared, referring to African Americans working to achieve equality and civil rights. It was popularized by Alain LeRoy Locke in 1925 in the anthology *The New Negro,* which promoted self-confidence and political activism by black intellectuals and earned him the title of "father of the Harlem Renaissance." The *Harlem Renaissance* was a movement of African American artists and intellectuals who celebrated the black culture that had emerged out of slavery and their cultural ties to Africa.

Although the word *tearjerker* for any sentimental movie, play, and so on goes back to 1921 (the synonym *weepie* was coined in Britain in 1928), most movies at that time were dramatic rather than mawkish, including such classics of the silent era as *Bleak House* (1922), *The Phantom of the Opera* (1925), and *Ben Hur: A Tale of the Christ* (1925). There was plenty of drama in real life as well, with the prevalence of crimes connected with Prohibition. The term *racketeer* was coined or popularized by *Time* magazine in 1928, just before the famous *St. Valentine's Day massacre* of February 14, 1929, which was masterminded by the racketeer Al Capone and in which seven men (six of them from the rival gang of "Bugs" Moran) were gunned down in a Chicago garage. But while the cities were shaken by rampant *gangsterism,* rural America had a religious revival as Protestant Christian churches were swept up by *fundamentalism,* with its emphasis on the literal truth of the Bible. The religious awakening created what came to be known as the *Bible Belt*, a large area in the South dominated by evangelism and revival meetings.

On·an economic level, the Roaring Twenties were fueled by a booming business climate. In 1925, a company called the Milestone Interstate Corporation announced that it planned to build and operate a chain of "motor hotels" between San Diego and Seattle, to be called "*Motel*," a word formed by blending *motor* and *hotel*. Long-distance travel across new *interstate* highways made motels necessities for motorists.

The top nonfiction bestseller of 1925 was Bruce Barton's *The Man Nobody Knows*, which presents Jesus as "the founder of modern business" and "the world's greatest business executive." The whole world was buying and selling, or engaging in stock market speculation, and it seemed that the sky was the limit. The heroic figure of Charles Lindbergh loomed large as an inspiration to millions who aspired to fame and riches. On May 20, 1927, Lindbergh, a hitherto obscure aviator, won instant world fame when he flew the first solo transatlantic flight from New York to Paris in his single-engine airplane, *The Spirit of St. Louis*. The *Lindy hop* (or *Lindy*), a dance that became popular the same year, was named after Lindbergh. Prosperity and optimism led to the landslide victory of the Republican candidate, Herbert Hoover, in the presidential election of 1928.

Then, in 1929, came a devastating letdown. The glorious ride of the 1920s ended with the catastrophic Wall Street stock market crash, recorded in history books as the *Great Crash of '29*. Years of rampant investment and speculation on the New York Stock Exchange had reached a crescendo, and suddenly stock prices began to fall precipitously. After three chaotic days, October 24 (*Black Thursday*), October 28 (*Black Monday*), and October 29 (*Black Tuesday*), the stock market collapsed and the grandiose dreams of millions of investors turned into a national nightmare.

A Selection of New Words of the 1920–1929 Decade

1920

adventurist, backsplash, beau geste, blooey, bongo, bootery, bozo, bunraku, bushwa, cartwheel (v.), chute, chutist, columnist, craftsperson, daiquiri, deb (= debutante), deflationary, delish, demob (v.), feedback, filmable, gaga, guacamole, hemorrhage (v.), hip, homophobia, icky, inflationary, jihadi, leftism, leotard, listenable, lovekins, mark-up, mappable, martial art, miscue (n.), mock-up, murderable, nah (adv.), nonviolence, nuanced, off-the-rack, opinionation, palooka, paranormal, periodontist, perk (= percolate), piña colada, plus fours, Ponzi scheme, proton, rabbit-punch (v.), rev (v.), ritzy, scenarist, skijoring, Steuben, subprime, sukiyaki, tempura, Tetrazzini, T-shirt, upgrade (v.), whee, wimp, wow, yippee, zing (v.)

1921

Alice-in-Wonderland (adj.), Americanologist, auto-suggest (v.), Bacardi, blankie, bouncy, carboxylation, Chaplinesque, checkup, Chekhovian, cold turkey, comparison shopping, cryptanalysis, dehumidify, déraciné, Dodgem, dog pile, envision, expressionistic, Fascism, Fascist, featherbedding, Gandhian, goalie, go-getter, goofy, goon, handedness, hicksville, kendo, kilocycle, Kiwanis, kolkhoz, Lincolniana, lo (= hello), Mary Jane (= low-heel shoe), machinability, man-haul (v.), maneuverable, Mare Nostrum, maternalism, nursemaid (v.), op (= operator), optionalize, ovenware, overblouse, ownsome, paramedical, pasticceria, pastism, peppiness, pin curler, pogo (v.), pogo stick, pollutional, postmodern, power play, prepster, pressure cooker, put and take, quadriplegic, razz (v.), saboteur, sadomasochistic, salchow, Shih-tzu, slalom, sovkhoz, stockpile (v.), supercharger, Tarzan, tearjerker, teenage, upstage (v.)

1922

arabica (coffee), banditry, beauty queen, beauty salon, bicarb, biracial, bistro, boîte, booboisie, botch-up, broadcaster, bug-eyed, chorine, decommission (v.), dimwit, downfield, dreck, duplex, entrepeneurial, escalate, farofa, fettucine, finalize, forehander, Formica, Gestalt psychology, gigolo, heinie, high-ranking, invitational, isolationism, jayvee, lamé, libidinal,

mah-jong, marocain, mass product, millisecond, misgauge (v.),
motorboat (v.), moviegoing (adj.), mudpack, no-brow, no
contest, notarize, notepad, off-tackle, one-shotter, oops (interj.),
operettist, ovenproof, passback, performative, photofit, photo-
offset, playset, Pollyannaish, polyester, prepper, pre-puberty,
puckster, pushmi-pullyu, putt-putt, roster (v.), rumba, schlep
(v.), shoot-up, sickle-cell anemia, sloganeer, sodbuster, step-in,
transvestite, tux, Uncle Tom, vacuum (v.)

1923

ace (v.), aerosol, Amerenglish, Babbitt, balletomane,
Bauhaus, Charleston, comfort zone, compartmentalization,
culturalize, debunk (v.), deplane (v.), dulce de leche, emplane
(v.), environmentalism, fag, fantasist, fictioneer, functionalize,
fundamentalism, heebie-jeebies, hijack (v.), hitchhike (v.),
hobohemia, Houdini, improvisational, intro, Jeez (interj.),
junkie, kayo (v., n.), mah-jong (v.), maneuverability, mantric,
mass media, mass-produce, mastectomy, media, microworld,
mobilize, moonchild, moviegoer, moviola, musclehead,
niftiness, nonjudgmental, noodle (v.), numerologist, nummy,
nutsy, off-again on-again, Politburo, popsicle, posh (n.),
prescreen (v.), pretest (n.), prop man, rainout, robot, run-
through, sax, schnauzer, shimmy (v.), sky-writing, sleep-
walk (v.), slenderize, sophisticate (n.), spotlight (v.),
360-degree (adj.), ultrasound, wham, whosis

1924

anorak, Appaloosa, automatization, Band-Aid, beautician, blah, blip (v.), constructivism, deregister, desorb, didgeridoo, duende, empathize, flub (v.), free-ranged, gimp, gotta, gravitas, headcount, high-hat (v.), hincty, ho-hum, hooey, hourage, house-train (v.), hype (= hypodermic), id, instinctual, interstate, kinkiness, Kleagle, Leftist, lumpenproletariat, luncheonette, magic bullet, malarkey, mash (v.), matriarchic, migrancy, misalignment, narrowcasting, naysaying, nevermind (n.), op (= operative), outpunch (v.), over-the-board, photocopy (v.), Piscean, pix, pressure group, pull tab, put-you-up, puzzlist, quantum jump, racketeer, radiocast (n., v.), scatological, sexpert, shush (v.), socko, stinko, stoolie, superego, swoosh, teletype, two-time (v.), uh-huh, uh-uh, voyeurism, wildcraft, wisecrack, wow (v.), yoo-hoo

1925

arachnophobia, Australopithecus, bail out, ball-hawking, cannoli, chewy, Comintern, compartmentalize, configurational, cosmic rays, coulda, cuppa, dis (adj., v.), dream team, Einsteinian, fink (v.), freebie, gavel (v.), giddap (v.), gimp, guppy, hightail (v.), introject (v.), Kleenex, knitwear, Leica, makeover, marathoner, middlebrow, moms (= mom), motel, mothproof (v.), needlepointer, neonate,

neurosurgeon, nudnik, OK sign, oncologist, pegity, pep
talker, pinboard, pointage, prosocial, puerilism, push-on,
quiche, referend, roadability, shamus, shashlik, sousaphone,
superstar, telephoto, twerp, Tootsie Roll, Trotskyism, twerp,
usherette, wham (v.), Wheaties, whoops, zipper

1926

airtime, angioplasty, attractant, bar-b-q, blooper, boosterism,
byline, cinéaste, claustrophilia, clementine, combo,
conformism, corgi, cosmetician, cosmetic surgery, co-star
(n.), crack-up, crispbread, cultish, demi-sect, dicty,
disaffiliation, downtrend, downturn, ear-bender, escapologist,
exclusivity, expandable, fantasize, finagle, fridge, Frigidaire,
gangdom, genome, geriatric, gig, gimmick, haute cuisine,
Heldentenor, holism, holistic, Hollywood, hormonal, hotsy-
totsy, hype (n.,v.), implementation, inexpertise, jazzman,
jughead, keynoter, kitsch, lesion (v.), Levis, lowlight (n.), mal
du siècle, mariage blanc, market research, Masonite, meals-
on-wheels, megacycle, metrization, mike (= microphone),
mojo, mootah, muggle, naturist, necrophilic, numerological,
nutritionist, offset (adj.), online, outsmart (v.), pastis, pep talk,
photoflash, photon, phys. ed., pin-fit (v.), prepack (v.), preset
(v.), pressure-cook (v.), prostie, punditry, quickie, recycle (v.),
skiffle, stop-and-go, submachine gun, totalitarian,
totalitarianism, tunesmith

1927

air-conditioned, Arkie, ballyhooist, bingo (interj.), build-up, card-carrying, Central Casting, cinematic, collaborative, copilot, cover-up, decaffeinate (v.), defroster, deviant (n.), digitalize, discussant, disfunctional, disinhibit, do-gooder, estrogen, Eurocentric, free-styler, gate-crasher, half-track, head-counting, heist (n.), infrastructure, interior design, kibitz, kibitzer, Kool-Aid, latke, lotsa, manscape, Mayday, meanie, microsurgery, minimalism, miscast (adj.), nappy (n.), nine-to-five (adj.), non-stick (adj.), obsessive-compulsive, off-white, oh yeah?, old age security, on-stage, paso doble, payload, pecking order, Pentecostalism, perm (n.), pit bull, pitchwoman, plasticize, poop out, prankster, preemie, premiere (v.), preservationist, racist (n., adj.), reflexology, robotize, Rorschach test, rub-out, short list, smash-and-grab raid, spin-dry (v.), Stalinism, stereophonic, strep throat, surrealism, tailspin (v.), televise, tigon, tomcat (v.), voguish, wearability, wing-ding, xylophonist

1928

abrazo, America Firster, athlete's foot, baloney (= humbug), barbiturate, bitchy, boogie-woogie, bottleneck (v.), breakfront, capoeira, clerihew, dead-pan (adj., n.), decibel, detainee, duplicable, eroticist, everyplace, exhibitionistic, Fascistic, girl

Friday, good neighbor (policy), good-time (adj.), hostess (v.), hunter-gatherer, hyperventilation, jammies, jive (n., v.), Jugendstil, liaise, line dancer, macher, macho, Mary Jane (= marijuana), moonquake, muckety-muck, newscast (v.), nite (= night), non-book, nut hatch, paper-pusher, perm (v.), pike dive, plastician, pockmark (v.), poop sheet, putz, quick-freeze (v.), racketeer (v.), roller-skate (v.), scampi, scram (v.), sexy, shoo-in (n.), snuggly, socialite, spray-paint (v.), Stalinist, switchover, tap-dancing, transvestism, upsurge, voguey

---

1929

after-school, ambisextrous, astronautics, beep, bi-level, ciao, cilantro, co-host (v.), do-si-do, dumb cluck, effing, esoterica, filmic, folksay, fuzz (= police), homie, homo, inhalator, inky, ixnay (adv.), jalopy, jeepers, klezmer, lame-brain, lifestyle, mariachi, Marxism-Leninism, means test, moom pitcher, nudism, nudist, obfuscatory, off-kilter, Oktoberfest, 101 (adj.), on-screen, overdrive, overpass, penicillin, photocomposition, pink lady, playback, polo neck, postdoctoral, post-op, pre-teen (adj., n.), prima-donna (v.), qwerty (adj.), rec (= recreation), Red-baiting, ref (v.), reroute (v.), sadomasochist, sasquatch, scat (singing), schm-, science fiction, shockability, show-jumping, sked (= schedule), sloganize, smoothie, sync, telemeter, teleprinter, tommy-gun, toughie, voyeuristic, whoop-de-do, Yanqui, zap, zucchini

Chapter 4

The Great Depression:

1930–1939

It was President Herbert Hoover who first applied the word *depression* to the economic collapse that followed the Crash of '29. In a message to Congress in December of 1930, he declared, "Economic depression cannot be cured by legislative action or executive pronouncement." Robert S. McElvaine, in his book *The Great Depression* (1984), explains: "The President . . . believed 'depression' had a less ominous ring to it than the more common previously used words 'panic' and 'crisis.'" But in the end, *depression* did take on an ominous ring and became so closely associated with the 1930s that the decade became known as that of the *Great Depression.*

The 1930s were the time of the *skid row* (1931), defined in A. J. Pollock's *Underworld Speaks* (1935) as a "district in a city where tramps (bums) congregate," of the shanty towns called *Hoovervilles* (1933, named after President Hoover) where the unemployed and their evicted families lived in tin and cardboard shacks, and of the *Dust Bowl* (1936), the vast prairie lands destroyed by drought that drove impoverished farmers from Oklahoma (*Okies*) and Arkansas (*Arkies*) to California and other states, as described in John Steinbeck's *The Grapes of Wrath* (1939). The popular song of 1931, "Happy Days

Are Here Again," turned by 1933 into "Brother, Can You Spare a Dime?"

In accepting his nomination as the presidential candidate of the Democratic Party in 1932, Franklin D. Roosevelt announced: "I pledge you, I pledge myself, to a new deal for the American people." The term *New Deal* became the name of the economic and social program implemented by the Roosevelt administration to counter the Depression; advocates of the New Deal were called *New Dealers*. The first measure of the New Deal presented to Congress was the euphemistically named *bank holiday*, when all banks were closed to prevent depositors from withdrawing their money. Other measures followed, creating what became known as the New Deal's *alphabet soup* of federal agencies (e.g., AAA, CCC, FDIC, FHA, NRA, SSA, WPA). The president's evening *fireside chats*, delivered nationwide by radio, helped publicize the New Deal programs and inspire public confidence in them.

The most popular humorist of those years, Will Rogers, pointed out that the way President Roosevelt explained banking to the folks at home, even bankers could understand. He once said, "The whole country is with him. . . . If he burned down the Capitol, we would cheer and say, 'Well, we at least got a fire started anyhow.'"

Disgust with Prohibition and the crimes it fostered reached its peak during the Great Depression. In March 1933 President Roosevelt signed into law an amendment (the Twenty-first Amendment) to the Volstead Act that effectively repealed Prohibition.

The decade of the 1930s was the golden age of radio. There was no network television yet. At the end of each day, families would settle down around the radio and listen to the news, to popular shows like *Amos 'N' Andy, Burns and Allen, Fibber McGee and Molly,* and *The Goldbergs. Soap operas,* so called because many were sponsored by soap and detergent companies, were introduced in 1930. A popular radio series for children was "Little Orphan Annie," in which Annie and her dog, Sandy, solved detective mysteries. Perhaps the most talked-about event in the history of radio was the October 30, 1938, broadcast of H. G. Wells's *War of the Worlds,* which dramatized a landing in New Jersey by invading Martians with such realism that shocked listeners took to the streets in what was described as mass hysteria. The next day, the *New York Times* ran the following front-page headline: "Radio Listeners in Panic, Taking War Drama as Fact. Many Flee Homes to Escape 'Gas Raid from Mars'—Phone Calls Swamp Police at Broadcast of Wells Fantasy." According to a study of the famous broadcast, conducted by a Princeton professor, more than six million listeners heard the tale of the invasion from Mars and an estimated 1.7 million people believed the radio play was real.

What radio was to the ears, newspapers were to the eyes. A major journalistic innovation of the '30s was the *op-ed page,* introduced by Herbert Bayard Swope (1882–1958), a legend among journalists. As correspondent for the *New York World* during World War I, Swope won a Pulitzer Prize in 1917 (the first year of the prizes) for a series of articles titled "Inside the German Empire." As executive editor of the *NYWorld* in the 1920s, Swope introduced new features in the newspaper, among them a distinctive page devoted to personal opinions by columnists, placed directly opposite the editorial page. "It occurred to me," he once wrote, "that nothing is more interesting than opinion when opinion is interesting, so I devised a method of cleaning off the page opposite the editorial . . . and thereon I decided to print opinions, ignoring facts." His colleagues on the paper soon began to refer to the page as the *op-ed*, a contraction of *opposite editorial.* The idea was not immediately copied by other newspapers, though it was admiringly referred to in 1931. It was not until the 1970s, when personal-opinion articles were often included in daily papers, that the *op-ed page* became a standard (now referred to as "traditional") feature of most newspapers.

To escape the gloom of the Depression, Americans turned to *escapism* (1933), the habit and practice of seeking distractions from everyday life. This took many forms. There were books, such as the best-selling novels of the decade: *The Good Earth* (1931), *God's Little Acre* (1933), *Gone with the Wind* (1936), and *The Grapes of Wrath* (1939), all of which focused on hope born out of despair. Self-help and success-promising books abounded; Dale Carnegie's *How to Win Friends and Influence People* (1936) was a sellout at 750,000 copies in its first year. There were the new *long-playing* phonograph records, whose length was all of fifteen minutes. There was *moviegoing*, which brought escapism to its zenith with the *screwball comedy,* a genre of breezy, satirical, and totally unrealistic films typified by *It Happened One Night* (1934), *Mr. Deeds Goes to Town* (1936), *Easy Living* (1937), and *You Can't Take It with You* (1938).

Some of these movies got *Oscars,* formally known as *Academy Awards,* consisting of gold-plated statuettes of a knight holding a sword and standing on a reel of film. The statuettes have been awarded yearly since 1928 by the Academy of Motion Picture Arts and Sciences (AMPAS), but the origin of the name *Oscar* is not certain. Claimants to having named the award include Bette Davis and Walt Disney. However, the *OED* notes that the name derives "perhaps" from *Oscar* Pierce, a wheat and fruit grower who was the uncle of Margaret Herrick, the Academy's executive director. In 1931, when Herrick first saw the statuette, she said that it reminded her of her "Uncle Oscar." Newspapers picked up the story, and in 1934 began to call the awards "Oscars." Both names, *Academy Award* and *Oscar,* are registered trademarks of AMPAS.

People also saved money by flocking to free-admission museums to view the latest works of artists, like the kinetic art of the sculptor and painter Alexander Calder, who introduced in 1932 the *mobile,* an abstract sculpture built of pieces of metal, plastic, and the like, suspended in midair so that its parts can move and rotate; an immobile version of it was named a *stabile* in 1943. Other forms of escapism were dancing the *jitterbug, rumba,* and *conga* to the sound of *jukeboxes,* which played recorded music at five cents a shot at bars, restaurants, and roadside dance joints; playing *bingo* or *Monopoly;* attending theater *revusicals* (part revue and part musical), such as the *Ziegfeld Follies;* and shopping at the newly opened *supermarkets,* one of which typically advertised itself in 1933 as "The 'One-stop-drive-in super market' provides free parking, and every kind of food under one roof."

Escapism took another form, a paradoxical admiration for the rich and their possessions. Every poor man's dream was to be a *Rockefeller,* alluding to the immensely wealthy financier John D. Rockefeller (1839–1937), who once said, "The good Lord gave me my money." One of the most popular songs of the time was "We're in the Money," from the film *Gold Diggers of 1933*:

> *We're in the money, we're in the money;*
> *We've got a lot of what it takes to get along!*
> *We're in the money, that sky is sunny,*
> *Old Man Depression you are through, you done us*
> *   wrong.*

Another pop song, "Life Is but a Bowl of Cherries" (1931), aimed for a calming effect on the impoverished citizens standing in breadlines and soup kitchens:

> *Life is just a bowl of cherries.*
> *Don't take it serious; it's too mysterious.*
> *You work, you save, you worry so,*
> *But you can't take your dough when you go, go, go.*

When Yiddish speakers in the United States, many of them immigrants or children of immigrants, began to assimilate into the great melting pot of America, they mixed into their English many Yiddish words and expressions that in 1933 became known as *Yiddishisms*. The 1930s were especially ripe with new words borrowed from Yiddish. Here is a sampling of Yiddishisms, arranged chronologically, that became Americanized in the 1930s:

mensch, n. [1930]. A good person; a decent, trustworthy human being. From Yiddish *mentsh*, literally, "human being."

knish, n. [1930]. A baked or fried dumpling filled with potatoes, kasha, cheese, etc. From Yiddish, from Polish *knysz*.

toches, n. [1930]. The buttocks, backside. From Yiddish *tokhes*, from Hebrew *tachat* "underneath."

yentz, v. [1930]. To cheat, swindle. From Yiddish *yentsn*, literally, "to fornicate." The use of this word, both in Yiddish and English, is vulgar; compare the slang verb *to screw*.

yenta, n. [1931]. A busybody or gossip. From Yiddish *yente*, originally a female name, shortened from *yentl*, a Yiddishized form of Old Italian *gentile* "genteel."

bagel, n. [1932]. A ring-shaped bread roll. From Yiddish *beygl*, apparently from dialectal German *beugel*, from the German root *beug-*, *boug-* "to bow, bend."

futz around [1932]. To mess around. Apparently from the Yiddish vulgarism *arumfartsn*.

pareve, adj. [1933]. (Of food) neutral; neither meat nor dairy. From Yiddish *pareve, parve*, probably of West Slavic origin (compare Czech *párový*, "dual," from *pár*, "pair").

schlepper, n. [1934]. A vagabond or beggar. From Yiddish *shleper*, from *shlepn* "to drag."

schmaltz, n. [1935]. Excessive sentimentalism, mawkishness. From Yiddish *shmalts*, literally, "fat."—*schmaltzy, adj.*

zaftig, adj. [1937]. Voluptuous, buxom. From Yiddish, literally, "juicy."

schmooze, n. [1939]. Idle conversation, chat. From Yiddish *shmues*, from Hebrew *shemuoth* "reports, news." The verb, *to schmooze* "to chat," was used in the 1920s.

Science and technology were not neglected in the 1930s. Here are some important terms that first appeared in the 1930s, listed alphabetically:

ecosystem [1935]. The basic unit of ecology, formed by the interaction of a group of organisms with its environment.

hydroponics [1937]. The cultivation of plants in liquid nutrient solutions.

mammogram [1937]. An X-ray of the breast for detecting tumors.

minicam [1936]. A miniature photographic camera. The term was applied to a small television camera in 1977.

Pilates [1934]. A system of exercises designed to improve physical fitness. Named after Joseph *Pilates* (1880–1967), who devised the system.

rocketry [1930]. The science of rocket propulsion. The word was coined at a meeting of the American Interplanetary Society in 1930.

spacecraft [1930]. A vehicle designed for travel in outer space.

television [1930]. The broadcasting of images by radio transmission. The term *television* was used in 1907 to mean a system for reproducing images at a distance on a screen.

telecast [1937]. A television broadcast.

video [1937]. The viewing channel in television as disinguished from the *audio* or sound channel.

Working its way through the Great Depression, America paid little attention to international developments in the 1930s, though there were signs of trouble ahead: the threats of *Agit-prop* (Russian Communist agitation and propaganda), *fellow travelers* (Communist sympathizers), *the fifth column* (secret traitors), and *show trials* (Communist trials of dissidents), alongside the rise of the *Nazis* (also known as *brownshirts* in 1932), with their *Aryan* ideology, their symbolic *swastika*, and their *Third Reich* (the "third Empire" led by Hitler). Nineteen thirty-eight paved the road to the war that would swamp the world in the 1940s. On March 13, 1938, Hitler accomplished by force the *Anschluss,* or annexation of Austria to Germany. On September 29, *Munich* entered the language as a disparaging synonym of submissive *appeasement* when the British prime minister, Neville Chamberlain, signed the agreement by which the Sudeten region of northern Czechoslovakia would be occupied by Germany. And on November 9, 1938, the pogrom of *Kristallnacht* ("the night of the shattered crystals") broke out, when Nazis destroyed synagogues, looted Jewish stores, and killed or arrested Jews throughout Germany, foreshadowing the Holocaust. On September 1, 1939, one week after signing a pact with the Soviet Union, Nazi Germany's *Luftwaffe* bombed major cities in Poland, marking the beginning of *World War II.* Within days of the invasion, Great Britain and France declared war on Germany, while the United States announced its neutrality. Following the German invasion, there were several months of the *Phoney War,* called in German *Sitzkrieg* ("sitting war"), during which little military activity occurred outside Poland. The real war, involving the major countries of the world, did not begin until the next decade.

A Selection of New Words of the 1930–1939 Decade

1930

airframe, air mobility, Alexander (cocktail), axel, balletomane, bass-ackwards, bathysphere, brucellosis, boff (v.), ceramicist, clonk (v.), coolant, crooner, derailleur, digoxin, doozer, downgrade (v.), drive-in, escapist, Fabergé, foodism, freeway, gangbuster, genome, go-slow, green card, grand jeté, handset, hood (= hoodlum), holster (v.), hostessy, hyperbaric, infrasound, interdiscipline, jingle, kinescope, knish, mensch, metagalaxy, mindscape, minoritarian, mixmaster, montage, moxie, Nazi, Nembutal, newscaster, noosphere, palsy (adj.), phytotoxic, pistol-whip (v.), PJs (= pajamas), poor-mouth (v.), press lord, pressure (v.), puppeteer, quick-freeze (v.), rocketry, schmeer, schnozzle, Sitzfleisch, snack bar, sociopath, spacecraft, strip-teaser, Third Reich, toches, trigger (v.), vibraharp, wee-wee, whodunit, zipper (v.)

1931

ailurophile (= cat lover), biennale, biggie, black market, black-top, bloop, bonk (v.), breezeway, camp (= exaggerate), carny, comparison shop (v.), courgette, double-park (v.), econometric, euthanize, filmlet, Filofax, fluorinate, flat out (adv.), gamesman, gemmologist, glossy (n.), high-octane, hoo-ha, hyperventilate (v.), infantilize, jitter (v.), judder (v.), kibbutz, Lotto, maladaptive, mass marketing, med (= medicine), mentholated, microwave, Monday-morning quarterback, motivational, moviegoing, National Socialism, nitwitted, on-off, op-ed, patch test, Pavlovian, pen pal, photomontage, platinum blonde, poor boy (sandwich), pop quiz, psych (v.), revusical, santero, sexual orientation, skid

row, snazzy, snowmobile, teleportation, thermosetting,
underpants, undersexed, water-ski (n., v.), widget, yenta

1932

Amerasian, aromaticity, Aryan, asymptomatic, bagel, baud,
born (v.), bruxism, burp (n., v.), caffeinated, cojones, crapper,
de-icer, demodulate, descale, devoice, eek (interj.), eight-
ball, electromatic, electron microscope, empathetic, fixer-
upper, free climber, Freon, futz (v.), gelato, goof (v.), gotcha,
green belt, gurk, hairdo, hangarage, Hebe, hopefully,
Intourist, iron lung, Juneteenth, kickback, layabout, lechayim,
lekach, logistically, malabsorption, malnourishment,
marinara, marvy, meltwater, microprobe, mouth bow,
Muslimization, mutual fund, narrowcasting, Nazism,
newsworthy, now-it-can-be-told, off-screen, okey-dokey, old
school tie, overpublicize, Pablum, Pentecostalism, phonon,
po' boy (sandwich), polyunsaturated, prefabricate, pricey,
psychodrama, put-down, radiosonde, reflation, reticulosis,
ritualization, simchah, skin-diver, smooch (v.), stumblebum,
telecommunication, telex, temp, toon, tweeze (v.), ultra-
high, unelectable, Ustashi, walkathon, write-in, yo-yo (v.)

1933

abseil, acte gratuit, airmobile, analysand, angiogram,
antihistamine, ascorbic acid, basenji, benzedrine, caffè

espresso, cell (= celluloid), Chrisake, clip-joint, co-driver,
comparatists, dagnabbit, diktat, discography, dumb down,
emcee, escapism, freeloader, free-styled, frottage, graph, ham
(v.), hetero, hi-octane, hydropower, Jacobethan, juke (v.),
Jungian, keypunch, kyudo, landsman, Loch Ness, magic
realism, maldistributed, mass market, mass observation, med
(= medical), Milquetoast, misorientation, moderne (adj.),
molly (fish), nabe, narratage, nightclubby, non-art, oink (v.),
oligopoly, overbudget (v.), pareve, pearlescence, peasanty,
pesticide, phoney baloney, pin-sharp, postflight, postgrad,
pre-op, pretzel (v.), proactive, pump-priming, queerie, racism,
reorient (v.), scaredy-cat, shoppe, shoulda, Spätzle, spot check,
staph, storm-trooper, supermarket, switcheroo, swingy,
tagmeme, tongue-in-cheek, Tudorbethan, tune-up, VIP

1934

aborning, Agit-prop, antioxidant, antipasto, anyplace,
archive (v.), articulacy, audio, ballerino, balletomania, boffo,
bonk (n.), booksy, Bouvier (dog), boxer (dog), brickette,
briefs (underpants), brutalist, bulgur, burrito, calypso, c'mon,
contaminant, contextualize, counsellee, customize, dagnab,
destabilize, deworm, dreidel, drunkometer, enrollee,
evacuee, expressivity, extrasensory, fetishize, Führer, gas up,
Gestapo, ginch, high fidelity, highlight (v.), Hispanist,
homegirl, impactive, inhale (n.), Jell-O, jitterbug (n.),

keynote (v.), Komsomol, lube (n., v.), mainliner, mealy-mouth (v.), mojito, Monopoly (game), neo-Communist, neo-fascist, neutrino, New Dealish, newscast, nitery, nudie, nutburger, nympho, okey-doke, one-off, Oscar (statuette), osso buco, Pilates, po-faced, Red China, referral, renegotiate, rerun, Roshi (Zen), routinier, schlepper, seismics, simonize, s'more, speedo (= speedometer), spillage, spiv, stinkeroo, supernova, tweeter, undercapitalize, uptight, weedicide, whistle-stop, woofer, yizkor, zesty

1935

air-to-ground, al dente, audition (v.), autodrome, autopilot, bazooka, bollix (v.), boondoggle, boysenberry, carry-out, centrism, codependent, commercial (n.), conga, crackdown, crew (v.), de-ice, dilly (n.), ecosystem, enduro, ex (v.), 4-H'er, foodist, freestyle (v.), gagster, geek (v.), gook, gravlax, haircare, Hammond organ, hasta la vista, hic et nunc (= here and now), hoke (v.), judder (n.), juke (n.), kwashiorkor, landrace, Luftwaffe, Magnum (gun), marriage guidance, mercy killing, meths, Mideast, mojo, monogram (v.), multicultural, multipurpose, Muzak, oink (interj.), osmolal, Pakistani, papillomavirus, paramilitary, Pentothal, photo finish, Plexiglas, prefinished, riboflavin, riff (n., music), scat (v., music), schmaltz, schmaltzy, script (v.), Seconal, shack-up, sitzmark, sleep-over, Stakhanovite, telephonitis, televiewer,

testosterone, thingism, Thanatos, tizzy, tour jeté, trahison des
clercs, venography, virology, wacky, Wehrmacht, Wimpy

1936

abubble, à la page, anti-abortion, aqua, back forty (acreage),
bathinette, beep (v.), B-girl, bingo, blabbermuth, bobby pin,
borscht circuit, bra, -cade (motorcade, etc.), cook-off,
curvaceous, decontaminate, demo, dino (= dinosaur), double
dip, dressage, dysfunctional, eighty-six (= nix), Exercycle,
fellow traveler, fifth column, flopperoo, frank (= frankfurter),
gang-up, gauleiter, ghetto (v.), glam, glamorize, guesstimate
(n.), harrumph, hi-de-ho (interj.), kishke, locatable, maker-
upper, male chauvinism, malinvestment, mansionette, marital
rape, Mata Hari, meld (v.), minicam, mocktail, modularize,
moral majority, mud-slogger, must-see, nice Nelly, nice
nellyism, nightclub (v.), niqab, Nobelist, nogoodnik,
nonevent, noodly, objet trouvé, outmigration, oversteer
(n., v.), pariahhood, pep-talk (v.), perc (= percolated coffee),
perfect storm, Phalangist, philo-Semitism, phonily, pickup
sticks, piggybacking, Pilipino (adj.), pit(t)a, pitch mark,
pixilation, plock (n.), Polaroid, Popular Front, porteur,
post-modernity, power-political, preem (= premiere),
prerecorded, prestigeful, prestressed, Rotavator, sablefish,
slap-happy, starry-eyed, steroid, striptease, surreal, sweet-talk
(v.), thataboy, toots, turnaround

1937

air-condition (v.), autobahn, baby-sitter, bomblet, Bren gun, calque, campesino, caplet, challah, cliffhanger, coagulant, debeak, dirndl, dumpster, embourgeoisement, ex ante, ex post, Falange, fibreglass, Francoist, freeloading, giant slalom, groovy, gunky, hobbit, hydroponics, iffy, interdisciplinary, invasiveness, I-Thou, Keynesian, lederhosen, leverage (v.), mammogram, mammography, marriage counseling, Marxist-Leninism, meltdown, microfilm (v.), minicam (v.), mirror symmetry, Mudville, news brief, oomph, palsy-walsy, pan-fry (v.), particle physics, party mix, payola, personal space, pidginize, pizzazz, prefab, presale, pro-am, race-baiting, Rasputin, rat race, rightist, rollback, schuss (n., v.), segue (n.), show trial, sit-in, smarm, Spam, spooked, subsonic, supremo, telecast (n.), tortellini, Turing machine, upfront, video, yeti, zaftig, zaibatsu

1938

Afro (adj.), ambisexual, amphetamine, baba ganoush, babushka, BBQ, break-even, bunny hop, cheeseburger, coq au vin, de-emphasize, deglamorize, disinvestment, double-take, double-talk, Dracula, drum-majorette, ept (adj.), escalation, expressway, fave, front end, gruntled, hep-cat, hype (v., = stimulate), itsy-bitsy, killer-diller, liger, lutz, mainline (v.), M.C. (v.), metascience, microfibril, misfile, Moral

Rearmament, moue (v., = pout), mud-wrestling, Mulligan (golf), nativization, Nescafé, nose count, nylon, oceanarium, open plan, outdoorsman, parenting, photojournalism, Potemkin (adj.), private eye, prole (adj.), pronatalist, pump-prime (v.), purgee, Rockefeller, rodenticide, roomette, rumba (v.), Runyonesque, senior citizen, Sadie Hawkins, senile (n.), superette, Taoiseach, thermonuclear, tween-age, up-do, winterize, wrap-up, xylorimba, yock (n., v., = laugh)

1939

accessorize, ack-ack, addictive, air-to-air, Asdic, ATP, banjax (v.), bicoastal, blitz (v.), Blitzkrieg, burger, celebutante, counterspy, Disneyesque, dognapping, fluoridization, empanada, home movie, infantilization, Ivy League, jitterbug (v.), jukebox, kineticism, knackwurst, L-dopa, Little League, macumba, malfunction, matjes herring, McGuffin, meson, mesosphere, Messerschmidt, Methedrine, Mittel-European, moolah, name-dropper, Naziphile, neurohormone, nisei, Oedipal, overachiever, PAC (Political Action Committee), piggy bank, plowback, pocketa-pocketa, poliovirus, pollee, pollster, pratfall, prayer meeting, pressure (v.), raunchy, recap (n.), rightism, schlep (n.), schmooze (n.), self-image, soap opera, sociolinguistic, spin-drier, stooge (v.), telegenic, tickety-boo, twelve step, unzip, vichyssoise, vocoder, Voltaic, walkie-talkie, weigh-in, year-round, Zyklon

Chapter 5

World War II and Postwar:

1940–1949

In the September 25, 1939, issue of *Time* magazine, an article under the heading "Blitzkrieger" summed up the Nazi invasion of Poland in two sentences:

> *The battlefront disappeared, and with it the illusion that there had ever been a battlefront. For this was no war of occupation, but a war of quick penetration and obliteration—Blitzkrieg, lightning war.*

Blitzkrieg was Hitler's way of implementing his *New Order* (*Neuordnung*), which William L. Shirer, in *The Rise and Fall of the Third Reich* (1950), described as "a Nazi-ruled Europe whose resources would be exploited for the profit of Germany, whose people would be made the slaves of the German master race and whose 'undesirable elements'—above all, the Jews, but also many Slavs . . . —would be exterminated. The Jews and the Slavic peoples were *Untermenschen*—subhumans," as compared with the German *Herrenvolk*, or master race.

The German words above foreshadowed a veritable Blitzkrieg of Germanisms. From 1940 on, the world was blitzed with German loanwords, many of which became all too familiar to English speakers: the *Wehrmacht* (German armed forces), behind which came the *Einsatzgruppen*, the mobile units of *Schutzstaffel* ("defense squadrons"), better known as the *S.S.* or *Waffen-S.S.* ("armed S.S.")—whose task was to eliminate the "undesirable elements" in the conquered populations. There was also the *Abwehr* (German intelligence agency), and the *Gestapo* (acronym for *Geheime Staats-Polizei,* "secret state police"), charged with rounding up Jews to make conquered areas *Judenrein* ("Jew-clean") or *Judenfrei* ("Jew-free") by transporting them to *Konzentrationslagern* (concentration camps) or *Vernichtungslagern* (extermination camps). Captured soldiers, in turn, were sent to a *Stalag* (a prison camp, contraction of German *Stammlager,* "main camp").

World War II (a name first found in print in 1939) dominated the first half of the 1940s decade. The military fighters and weapons used in the war included the *Messerschmitt* fighter planes of the *Luftwaffe* (German air force), the American *Sherman tanks,* the *Spitfire* of the *R.A.F.* (British Royal Air Force) and its *Flying Squadrons,* the German *U-boats* (from German *U-boot,* abbreviation of *Unterseeboot* "undersea boat," i.e., submarine), the German *Stuka* dive-bomber, the *napalm* used in *flamethrowers,* the *Molotov cocktails* (incendiary devices named after V. M. Molotov, Soviet foreign minister), the Czech *Bren gun* and the British *Sten* submachine gun, the German *Panzer* tanks, and the American *amtracs* (amphibious tractors), used for landing assault troops—among many others.

On the domestic front, the entry of women into the

workforce found a popular symbol in *Rosie the Riveter*, who represented the millions of women who joined in the *war effort*, which included knitting socks and sweaters to keep the soldiers warm. On the war front, *G.I.s* went to the nearest *USO* center for entertainment or pinned pictures of attractive, scantily clad *pin-up girls* on the walls of their barracks. A 1941 issue of *Life* magazine reported: "[The actress] Dorothy Lamour was the No.1 pin-up girl in the U.S. Army." Another popular symbol, introduced by Winston Churchill, was the *V-sign* made with the fingers to show the letter *V* for victory.

Abbreviations used as words became commonplace during the war years. It's not known who coined the word *acronym* for wordlike abbreviations like *MASH* (Mobile Army Surgical Hospital), *radar* (*ra*dio *d*etecting *a*nd *r*anging), *SIGINT* (*Sig*nals *Int*elligence), and *UNESCO* (United Nations Educational, Scientific, and Cultural Organization). What's known is that *acronym* was an important World War II coinage, inspired by the proliferation of such pronounceable initialisms as *WAC* (Women's Army Corps), *WAVES* (Women Accepted for Volunteer Emergency Services), *jato* (*j*et-*a*ssisted *t*akeoff), *loran* (*lo*ng-*ra*nge *n*avigation), and *SHAEF* (Supreme Headquarters Allied Expeditionary Force—pronounced "shayf"). One view holds that *acronym* was coined by scientists at the U.S. Bell Laboratories, but that hasn't been confirmed. The coinage, formed from *acro-* "end, tip" + *-onym* "name" (ultimately from Greek), was clearly modeled on other words with *acro-* (like *acropolis* and *acrostic*) and *-onym* (like *synonym* and *antonym*).

An interesting acronym of the 1940s was *Seabees*. The name was chosen by the U.S. Navy in 1942 for members of its Construction Battalion as a fanciful alteration of the abbreviation *C.B.* for *Construction Battalion*. Someone in the navy read the abbreviation as "Sea Bee," and presto!, an insignia was created for the battalion: a flying, fighting bee wearing a sailor hat and armed with a firing submachine gun, a wrench, and a hammer. Practically overnight C.B. members became known as the Seabees. The closest example of a similar 1940s coinage is *Jeep*. First recorded in 1941 as the name of a small army vehicle with a four-wheel drive, it was created as a word from the abbreviation *G.P.* for *General Purpose*; the spelling *Jeep* is said to have been inspired by the name of "Eugene the Jeep," a cartoon character that "could go anywhere" but could only say the word *jeep,* introduced in 1936 in the comic strip "Popeye the Sailor" by the cartoonist E. C. Segar.

A curious acronym that arose from the 1930s "alphabet soup" of the New Deal was *Fannie Mae*, a creative name for *FNMA* (Federal National Mortgage Association), a government agency that in 1968 was converted to a private corporation. To expand the secondary mortgage market monopolized by Fannie Mae, in 1970 Congress created the *FHLMC* (Federal Home Loan Mortgage Corporation), which was promptly christened *Freddie Mac*. The acronyms stuck, totally replacing the abbreviations. During the financial crisis of September 2008, the government again took control of the two ailing mortgage giants in a gigantic bailout effort to save the U.S. economy.

The commonest abbreviation to emerge from WWII was *G.I.* for an enlisted member of the United States armed forces. Originally, *G.I.* was the abbreviation of *Government Issue,* a designation applied to equipment used by servicemen, as in *G.I. shoes, G.I. soap, G.I. trucks.* In the early 1940s, the abbreviation was broadened to include anything associated with servicemen (e.g., *a G.I. haircut, G.I. brides*). By 1943 *G.I.* became synonymous with "a U.S. soldier." The most important government education and readjustment program for returning veterans was the *G.I. Bill,* passed into law in 1944 and since then renewed in various forms. A famous synonym for an American soldier is *G.I. Joe,* which is also the name of the most popular military action figure in toy history.

A word borowed from Chinese attained wide currency during the war. The word was *gung-ho.* To be *gung-ho* means to be exceptionally enthusiastic, eager, or zealous, as in "Insurers too gung-ho on global warming" (*Miami Herald* headline). The word was introduced in 1942 as a training slogan by a U.S. Marine officer, Major Evans F. Carlson (1896–1947), from Chinese *kung ho* "work together." The phrase was an alteration of *gōng hé,* an abbreviated name of *gōngyè hézuòshè* "industrial workers cooperative," a cooperative established in rural China in 1938. The Chinese phrase was clipped to form the motto or slogan meaning "work together" for the industrial cooperative movement. Major Carlson picked up the slogan while traveling in China, and after he used it in commanding the second Marine Raider Battalion, *gung-ho* spread throughout the U.S. Marine Corps. It was then popularized by a 1943 war movie titled *Gung Ho!*, which told the story of a successful Marine Corps attack in 1942 on Japanese forces on Makin Island in the South Pacific.

The most memorable name emerging from World War II was a fictional one, *Kilroy*. The name sprang up suddenly in 1945 and was popularized by U.S. servicemen through inscriptions left on walls, sidewalks, ice, and so on, mainly in such phrases as "Kilroy was here" and "Kilroy slept here." The inscription often appeared alongside a sketch of a man's head with a long nose peeping over a wall that he clutches with both hands. Many accounts of the name's origin have been proposed, the most persistent one attributing it to a shipyard inspector named James J. Kilroy, who during World War II chalked his name on the bulkheads of newly constructed ships to show that he had inspected the riveting. To the troops, Kilroy became the mysterious G.I. who "was always there first"; hence, scrawling the catchphrase "Kilroy was here" wherever they went became a kind of signature of their presence. The name Kilroy still turns up in allusion to the wartime myth.

The most infamous word to arise during the war was *quisling,* used since 1940 to denote someone who aids or collaborates with an enemy invading force, a traitor. The word was an eponym, derived from the name of Vidkun *Quisling* (1887–1945), a Norwegian army officer, politician, and leader (*Fører*) of the Nasjonal Samling ("National Unity") fascist political party of Norway. After Germany invaded Norway in 1940, Quisling tried to become the head of a pro-Nazi government, a position he achieved in 1942. Following Germany's defeat in 1945 he was tried for high treason, convicted, and executed by a firing squad. "For the great majority of Serbs, he [Zoran Djindjic] will be remembered as a quisling who enriched himself by selling his country to those who had waged war against it so mercilessly only a few years earlier." (*The Guardian*, March 14, 2003)

Several important words were coined by individuals during the 1940s. Normally, coinages are like inventions: they either catch on, become hits, or bomb, die aborning. The word *genocide*, meaning the systematic extermination of an ethnic, national, or cultural group, struggled for four years to be universally accepted. The word was coined by a Polish Jewish lawyer, Rafael Lemkin (1900–1959), who in a 1944 book, *Axis Rule in Occupied Europe*, documented Nazi atrocities and gave it a name:

> *New conceptions require new terms. By "genocide" we mean the destruction of a nation or of an ethnic group. This new word, coined by the author to denote an old practice in its modern development, is made from the ancient Greek word* genos *(race, tribe) and the Latin* cide *(killing)....* *Generally speaking, genocide does not necessarily mean the immediate destruction of a nation, except when accomplished by mass killings of all members of a nation ...*
>
> *Genocide is directed against the national group as an entity, and the actions involved are*

directed against individuals, not in their individual capacity, but as members of the national group.

After the war, Lemkin worked tirelessly to make *genocide* a part of international law, finally succeeding in 1948, when on December 9 of that year the United Nations approved the "Convention on the Prevention and Punishment of the Crime of Genocide."

Another prominent technical coinage of the 1940s was *cybernetics.* Meaning "the operation and control of complex communication systems," *cybernetics* was coined in 1948 by the U.S. mathematician Norbert Wiener (1894–1964), the author of *Cybernetics, or Control and Communication in the Animal and Machine* (1948). Wiener created the word from a Latinate form of Greek *kybernétēs* "steersman, pilot" (from *kybernān* "to steer," the ultimate source of English *govern*) + the suffix *-ics.* Over time, the study of cybernetics produced new disciplines in various fields, such as *biocybernetics, psychocybernetics,* and *sociocybernetics,* but its greatest influence was on the emerging science of electronic computers. The combining form *cyber-* became descriptive of anything involving computers, as in *cyberspace* (the realm of computer systems), *cyberphobia* (an irrational fear of computers), and *cyberpunk* (a genre of science fiction based on cybernetics). Derivatives of the word include *cybernetic, cyberneticist,* and *cybernation.*

A more spontaneous coinage was the technical term *googol,* the name for the number 1 followed by 100 zeros, or 10 to the 100th power. The word was coined in 1940 by a nine-year-old boy, Milton Sirotta, the nephew of the U.S. mathematician Edward Kasner (1878–1955). According to Kasner, when he asked his young nephew to think up a name for a very big number, a number with a hundred zeros after it, Milton, after a moment's thought, answered "a googol!" Though probably influenced by the name of the then very popular comic-strip character Barney *Google,* Milton's coinage became important in advanced mathematics, spawning such terms as *googolplex* (1 followed by a googol of zeros) and *googolpolygon* (a polygon with a googol sides). The computer search engine *Google* was named by its inventors as a play on (or some would say a misspelling of) *googol,* by which they intended to suggest their objective of organizing the information on the World Wide Web to encompass googol-like amounts.

Another original and somewhat similar-sounding coinage of the '40s was *gobbledygook,* popularly applied to pretentious official jargon, as of bureaucrats. The word was coined in 1944 by a Texas lawyer and congressman, Maury Maverick Jr. (1921–2003), who defined it as "talk or writing which is long, pompous, vague, involved, usually with Latinized words." When asked how he conceived the word, he answered: "I do not know. It must have come in a vision. Perhaps I was thinking of the old bearded turkey gobbler back in Texas, who was always gobbledy gobbling and strutting with ludicrous pomposity. At the end of this gobble was a sort of gook."

The war in Europe ended in victory for the Allies on May 8, 1945 (*V-E Day*). For Americans the war ended on

September 2, 1945 (*V-J Day*), when Japan surrendered after *atom bombs* devastated Hiroshima and Nagasaki.

The war's end marked the start of the postwar baby boom, which produced in the United States about seventy-six million babies in the next eighteen years. The war had put an end to the Great Depression and ushered in a period of commercial and technical growth. The modern electronic digital *computer* made its debut in 1946 with the introduction of the *Eniac* (*Electronic Numerical Integrator and Computer*), the first general-purpose electronic computer, by the U.S. Army's Ballistic Research Laboratory. Advent of the electronic computer brought along new terms that are now standard: *program* (list of instructions for a computer), *data, hardware, memory, storage, bit* (binary digit). In 1947, a Hungarian-born British scientist, Dennis Gabor, invented *holography*, the production of three-dimensional images (*holograms*). The first *bathyscaphe*, a submersible vessel for deep descent into oceans (named from Greek *bathys* "deep" + *skaphos* "ship"), was built by the French scientist Auguste Piccard. Other postwar inventions included the *transistor*, the basic component of electronic devices, created by scientists of the Bell laboratories, and the fastener *Velcro*, invented by the Swiss mountaineer George de Mestral. *Antibiotics*, such as *actinomycin* and *neomycin* (isolated from a species of streptomyces), became widespread, though not yet as much as the *sulfa* drugs, which had proved to be invaluable in saving lives during the war.

In popular culture, *disk jockeys* plugged music for the latest dances, which included *boogie*, a style of blues based on the *boogie-woogie* of the 1930s, and *bebop*, a type of jazz also called *bop* for short. A more inclusive term, *rhythm and blues*, was introduced in 1949 by *Billboard* magazine as an umbrella term for African American music. A fad of the times was the *zoot suit*, a high-waisted, wide-legged suit with wide lapels and wide padded shoulders, worn by men to dances and parties; the suit was popularized by African American and Hispanic *hipsters*. Another much-publicized vogue was the sighting of *flying saucers*, or unidentified flying objects, first reported in 1947 by an American businessman who claimed to have seen nine disk-shaped objects flying in a chain near Mount Rainier, Washington. Many others confirmed similar sightings in the 1950s of what came to be known as UFOs. In transportation, the Volkswagen *Beetle* (German *Käfer*), a 1948-model economy car, also nicknamed the *Bug* for its rounded body and compact design, became the most popular means of terrestrial travel in the 1940s.

Perhaps the most talked-about innovation of the postwar years was the *bikini*. This word for a very brief two-piece bathing suit was borrowed in 1948 from French, which named the bathing suit in allusion to the large explosion that took place on *Bikini*, an atoll on the Marshall Islands where a nuclear weapon was tested in July of 1946. It was coined by the garment's designer, Louis Réard, to suggest that the excitement the skimpy suit would cause on the beaches would be akin to a nuclear explosion. Réard also coined *monokini*, a one-piece bikini made especially for men, contrasting *mono-* ("one, single") with *bi-* in *bikini*, as though this *bi-* was the prefix meaning "two," a clever pun, since the bikini is in fact a *two*-piece suit. The pun was topped in the 1960s, when a designer came up with the *trikini*, a three-piece bikini, consisting of a bottom piece and separate pieces for each breast. There seemed to be no room on the body for a four-piece item, so no *"quadrikini"* evolved.

The postwar years encouraged achievement in the performing arts. *Tony* is the name of a medallion awarded annually since 1947 by the American Theatre Wing for distinguished achievement in the American theater. Officially called the *Antoinette Perry Awards for Excellence in Theatre*, the Tonys were named after the nickname of *Antoinette* Perry (1888–1946), a U.S. actress, director, and cofounder of the American Theatre Wing. Another award, the *Emmy*, has been given annually since 1949 by the Academy of Television Arts and Sciences for excellence in television programming, production, and performance. A diminutive of *Emma*, the name *Emmy* is said to have been chosen because of its resemblance to *Immy*, a nickname of the *image orthicon* tubes used in the early television cameras. The Emmys, considered the television equivalent of the movie industry's *Oscars*, are also, like the latter, statuettes—but because of their female name, the statuettes are in the form of a winged woman holding up a large, globular atom, the wings symbolizing the "Arts" and the atom the "Sciences" of television.

With the Second World War over, the *Free World* (a Cold War term for the non-Communist nations) was free to engage in pursuits other than military conflict. President Truman announced in January 1949 his *Fair Deal* plan (modeled on Roosevelt's *New Deal*) to expand social security and other social programs. In April, the *North Atlantic Treaty Organization (NATO)* was established. The midcentury was poised to usher in a period of tranquility and affluence.

A Selection of New Words of the 1940–1949 Decade

1940

airlanding (adj.), avocational, baby blues, ball-hawk (v.), basho (sumo wrestling), beat-up, bicultural, bird-dog (v.), blitz (n.), bollocks (interj.), borscht belt, bounceback (n.), call-up, clamp-down, Commie, counterintelligence, crud, deemphasis, discophile, ecdysiast, extraordinaire, freeload (v.), Gallup poll, googol, gussy (v.), hiya (interj.), in-basket, interbellum, intercom, itty-bitty, laulau (dish), lesbo, ludic, mabe pearl, Mae West, male chauvinist, marginalization, Marxize, mayo, me-too (v.), midfielder, misallocation, mobile home, moola(h), must reading, no-growth (adj.), nosey (v.), out-basket, packaway, pair bond, paisan, paratroops, party-liner, pasta fazool, pendejo, phoney (v.), plea bargaining, poot (v.), pratfall (v.), pre-teener, primitivize, prisonize, privatize, pundit (v.), puppeteer (v.), put-up-or-shut-up (adj.), quisling, rank-and-filer, retsina, roadblock, schnozz, screen shot, Scrooge, shazam, Sieg Heil, skycap, Stepin Fetchit, super-duper, tape recording, telecast (v.), whammy

1941

add-on, airland (v.), apparatchik, astrodome, at-bat, back-and-forth (n.), bad-mouth (v.), beddable, bidirectional, butch, callback, cheesesteak, clipper (v.), corpsman, daisy-chain (v.), Daliesque, deep freeze, disk jockey, existentialism, exploitee, faux-naïf, free-associate (v.), FYI, game plan, Gaullist, goo (v.), gremlin, hipster, hummable, inductee, in-tray, jam-up, jazzophile, jeep, joe (= coffee), juvie, lease-lend, lend-lease, loud-hailer, Lou Gehrig's disease, lox (= salmon), majorette, malfunction (v.), marriage counselor, mastermind (v.), micromodel, multi-ethnic, mutie (= mutant), New Critic, New Criticism, normless, noshing, off-beam, Old Left, opener-upper, outslick, panpot, pansyish, paratrooper, pedalo, pedophile, peep (small jeep), perfecto, Piltdowner, pin-up girl, pisher, planeful, potty, prepone (v.), prerecord, preset, punchline (v.), radar, recce, rejectee, rematch, robotic, roll-on, second-guess (v.), Shangri-La, snafu, teen-ager, USO (United Service Organization, founded in 1941), welfare state, ya (pron.), yardbird, yee-haw (interj.)

1942

abortee, arty, ballsy, biog, blind copy, bottom-up, brownout, carb, car pool, cruzeiro, dike/dyke, dim-out, dojo, ear-bending, featurette, free-form, fud, Geronimo!, girlie man, globality, gung-ho, hyper (adj.), ick (interj.), indie, in like Flynn, in-migrant, in-migration, jeep (v.), market forces, momism, multivitamin, no-no, nutty (n.), paraglider, perv (n.), petrochemical, pistol-whip (v.), postdoc, privatization, Quonset hut, ramjet, red-out, self-medication, sexercise, sexploitation, simpy, slap shot, slash-and-burn (adj.), smack (= drug), smackeroo, smoke-jump (v.), smooch (n.), sockeroo, spelunker, spiceless, spiedie, stake-out, stats, strobe, sulfa, tech (= technician), trance dancer, the usual suspects, whatchamacallit, whiteout, winkle out, zap (v.), zoom (interj.), zoot suit

1943

acronym, adage (ballet), air freight (v.), beanie, bivvy (v.), bobby sock, boffo (adj., n.), cannibalize, carry-cot, changeup, chicken (v.), chino, choreograph, conveyorize, D.D.T., debark, defoliant, defuse, dog-and-pony (adj.), duh, eff (v.), fly-in, falsies, G.I., gizmo, jerrican, Kierkegaardian, Laundromat, localitis, loran, loud-hail (v.), maintainability, mestizaje, microfiche, middle-ager, mimeo, mod (= modification), mothball (v.), Motor City (= Detroit), neo-fascism, no-hoper, nucular, off-board, out-tray, pantsing, participational, passéism, patrilineality, patrilocally, pattern-bomb (v.), permafrost, phillumenist, plinker, poochie, posterize, pot-shotting (adj.), pranksterism, preliteracy, pretrain (v.),

race-bait (v.), ratio (v.), recce (v.), sad sack, scapegoat (v.),
sociodrama, spelldown, strategize, supergroup,
Weimaraner, yachtie

1944

absent (prep.), aerosolize, amtrac, angst, ball-busting, bear-
hug (v.), bluerinse, boondock, bremsstrahlung, brise-soleil,
busty, carpet bombing, clobber (v.), con (= convention),
consumerism, death camp, denazify, depressurize, deviance,
DNA, echolocation, ethnophaulism, fatso, freeze-drying,
fubar (interj.), genocide, gobbledygook, he-said-she-said,
hubba-hubba, imagineer (v.), infiltrator, jato, juvey,
leachable, Madison Avenue, mandlen, maquisard, metalegal,
microcard, microstate, mortar (v.), motorbike (v.),
multidisciplinary, neo-Nazi, numero uno, optimality,
palletized, paradoctor, parastatal, Pentagonese, permanent
press, personhood, pindown, planetfall, plastic bomb,
pochismo, pocho, pool driver, P.R. (= public relations),
prepackage (v.), pressurize, radome, returnee, schmendrick,
snorkel, Stateside, superpower, tag-along, vegan, walk-
through, wolf whistle, zillion, zubrowka (vodka)

1945

anti-g, anti-gravity, atom bomb, auditionee, automagically,
baby-sit, bebop, boff, bonkers, chugalug (v.), cockamamie,

cold war, comme ci comme ça, contrail, debrief, debug, decriminalization, doh (interj.), downscale (v.), Eisenhower jacket, espresso, existentialist, facticity, fifo, fissionable, frat (v.), frogman, gangbang (n.), glop, G-suit, hadda (= had to), helzapoppin, hokey, hot rod, inflight, Kahlua, Kilroy, lifo, link-up, map-read (v.), matricentric, microsleep, misroute, mixed media, mobile phone, moisturize, moldy fig, must-read (n.), name-dropping, natch, Nessie, New Critical, no-parking, nuclear bomb, open-endedness, over-the-road (adj.), passive-aggressive, pataphysics, patch testing, penny-pinch (v.), phaser, pit bull terrier, pre-cut, preload, redeploy (v.), repple-depple, retiree, roll-over, Sabra, sansei, schizo, sealant, shapka, show biz, Skybus, sonobuoy, squawk box, stack-up, sweet talk, swiftie, Teflon, tostada, videogenic, viewscreen, Vizsla (sporting dog), weaponeer, youthify

1946

backdate (v.), backlist, beeper, biscotto, boffola, bracero, Brooklynese, circuitry, clitoral, Cold War, counterfactual, crypto, dieselize, disincentive, Eames chair, ear-bending, Eniac, fast-talk (v.), flack, flightseeing, forint, fubar (v.), futurology, genotype (v.), gray market, Gulag, iconicity, instantiate (v.), Iron Curtain, Jaycee, jet (v.), junky, kerfuffle, koan, Latino, manicotti, Mariological, Marxist, massification, megabuck, metal detector, mickey (v.), microdot, microprocessing, miniaturize, misdiagnosis, miticide, mitogen, move-in, multicolored, nuclear power, oater, on-again off-again, orbit (v.), overkill (v.), palletization, pansy (v.), Peronism, physiatrist, pointy-head, porkchopper, preset, polyphonal, provolone, psych (n.), quadplex, radioisotope, rawin, rawinsonde, readout, repro, skimobile, Sno-cat, snooperscope, sonar, square (= conventional), subroutine, trishaw, tween, typecast (v.), weatherize, wilco

1947

afterburner, aftosa, apartheid, automaker, Benelux, bioactive, biocide, bop (v.), boson, Caesar salad, check-in, Chicano, Cominform, connotational, cookout, copter, corporatize, cosmonautical, daven, decartelization, deltiology, Disneyfied, dogpile (v.), ethnolinguistics, euphoriant, flying saucer, free-float (v.), Free World, gamesmanship, holography, honcho, hydrogen bomb, jet stream, Kafkaesque, keypunch (v.), leaseback, lookalike, Mahlerian, methadone, microanalytic, miniaturization, minimalistic, morph, multi-copy, multilateralist, Nacht und Nebel, name-dropper, neo-Keynesian, New Look, off-center, particle physicist, pass-fail, physiatry, pin-striper, playtest, rem (roentgen equivalent man), rupiah, Scotch tape, snowblade, switch-off, strobe (v.), terrorist, Tony, upbeat, Vietnamese, Walter Mitty, Wonderbra

1948

airlift (v.), automation, bakeware, bartend (v.), Beetle, bikini,
bit (= binary digit), bogey (v.), Bug, canasta, cappucino, co-
author (v.), cybernetics, Deutsche mark, dim sum, Dixiecrat,
ecopolitical, ecumenism, fax (n., = facsimile), GATT
(General Agreement on Tariffs and Trade), genocidal,
heliport, hoteling, idiolect, Lysenkoism, machismo, mambo,
Mariologist, mbira, Meso-American, microgroove, minicar,
miticidal, museumobile, nachos, namaste, narrowband,
NASCAR (National Association for Stock Car Auto Racing),
nativize, oddball, one-worlder, Orlon, paper-pushing,
pedicab, paradrop (n.), patzer, penlight, pesticidal, photo
essay, poetese, pre-wired, protoplanet, radarscope, radio
astronomy, rehab. RNA, retrorocket, Sartrean, schlimazel,
schlump, schmo, schnook, shmoo, simulcast (v.), Slinky,
smasheroo, soul-searching, tee (= T-shirt), transistor, TV,
tweener, update (v.), viral, won ton, work-up, zingy

1949

aromatherapy, bake-off, Bantustan, Big Brother, colorcast,
Comecon, Coxsackie virus, cruddy, daddy-o, deep-freeze (v.),
desalinate, DNase, dolorimeter, doublethink, dragon lady,
Dramamine, drive-through, Emmy, Fair Deal, fanzine, fiche,
flavonoid, genetic engineering, Ghanaian, gray area, home
perm, immobilism, jalapeño, kibbutznik, laundrette, Little

Leaguer, makeout, Maoist, maraboutism, matrilineage, maximin, me-tooism, muscle relaxant, NATO, Negritude, neomycin, neuropharmacology, Newspeak, nose cone, Olivetti, postmodern, pretest (v.), pro-am, quiche, rheumatology, rhythm and blues, Ritalin, rocketsonde, sail-off, scroungy, self-fulfilling, shtetl, slurp, supercalifragilisticexpialidocious, supergene, taco, tectonism, teevee, telethon, transduce (v.), tweenager, veep, welfarism, zydeco

Chapter 6

Midcentury—The Affluent Fifties:

1950–1959

When President Harry Truman addressed the United Nations in San Francisco on September 4, 1951, his speech was transmitted by television to viewers as far away as New England, marking the start of intercontinental television in the United States. Television was still so new to the public that it was an easy target of radio comedian Fred Allen, who on December 17, 1950, on the radio program *The Big Show,* quipped: "Television is the new medium. It's called a medium because nothing is well-done." He is also quoted in David Halberstam's book *The Fifties* (1993) as calling television "a device that permits people who haven't anything to do to watch people who can't do anything." At first a black-and-white medium, within three years the networks acquired color. Some of the popular early shows were the musical *Your Hit Parade* (1950–59), the comedy series *Our Miss Brooks* (1952–56), the cowboy series *The Gene Autry Show* (1950–56), and the children's show *Captain Kangaroo* (launched in 1955).

The 1950s, coming on the heels of the most devastating war in history, became the age of normalcy and conformity, of the pursuit of comfort and wealth, and of mass consumerism and general affluence. Indeed, the title of John Kenneth Galbraith's book *The Affluent Society* (1958) entered the language as describing the high level of economic well-being enjoyed by postwar society. The increase in the American birthrate resulting from the economic boom was dubbed the *Baby Boom,* a term that the columnist Sylvia F. Porter helped popularize in "Babies Equal Boom" (May 4, 1951), where she wrote: "Take the 3,548,000 babies born in 1950. Bundle them in a batch, bounce them all over the bountiful land that is America. What do you get? Boom. The biggest, boomiest boom ever known in history."

But not all was peaches and cream in the America of the '50s. The *Korean War,* which lasted three years (1950–53), cost over thirty-three thousand American lives. A term emerging from the treatment of prisoners during the Korean War was *brainwashing,* a method of systematically altering a person's attitudes and beliefs, especially through psychological manipulation. The term is a translation of Chinese *xi nao* ("to wash the brain"). The back-formed verb *to brainwash* appeared in 1953. The term was popularized by the 1959 novel (and subsequent motion picture) *The Manchurian Candidate,* in which a group of American soldiers imprisoned during the Korean War in 1952 are brainwashed, with tragic consequences. "The punishments meted out to Falun Gong practitioners . . . include forced brainwashing" (*The Epoch Times,* November 30, 2005).

The *Cold War* between the United States and the Soviet Union intensified during the 1950s, touching off the nuclear arms race and a new "*Red Scare*" (fear of espionage by Communists). The term *McCarthyism* came to mean the practice of publicly accusing individuals of engaging in subversive Communist activities, or, more generally, of disloyalty or treason to the United States, without evidence to substantiate the charges. The term was derived from the name of Joseph R. *McCarthy* (1909–1957), the U.S. Republican senator who between 1950 and 1954 aggressively investigated and accused supposed Communists of subversive activities. Here is a recent use of the term: "In the 1950s the right wing attacked liberals as being communists. In 2005 Karl Rove has attacked liberals as being therapists. Thus is born a kinder and gentler form of McCarthyism" (E. J. Dionne Jr., "The New McCarthyism," *Washington Post*, June 28, 2005).

Perhaps to block out the ever-present menace of nuclear war, Americans sought escape in an ever-expanding popular culture. In music, *doo-wop*, a genre of rhythm and blues, dominated the airwaves in the early '50s, to be soon eclipsed by *rock 'n' roll*, a form of popular music derived in part from blues and folk music and marked by a strong backbeat and a catchy melody. Though the term appeared originally (as *rock and roll*) in the lyrics of rhythm-and-blues songs in the 1940s, it was popularized in 1951 by the disc jockey Alan Freed, who played recordings of the music before large audiences in Cleveland, Ohio. The phrase *rocking and rolling* had been used since the 1920s in Black English slang as a euphemism for sexual relations, and even earlier as a term describing the motions of church dancing. A "white" type of rock 'n' roll, developed in the mid-1950s by singers like the teenage idol Elvis Presley and Jerry Lee Lewis, came to be known as *rockabilly* (a blend of *rock 'n' roll* and *hillbilly*), since it drew on both country music and rhythm and blues. Rock 'n' roll attained world fame after the song "Rock around the Clock" by Bill Haley & His Comets was played over the opening credits of *Blackboard Jungle,* a 1955 film about teachers and students in an inner-city school.

Disc jockeys playing records of rock 'n' roll on radio and in discotheques became so well known that they came to be called *deejays* for short. The term was first recorded in Leonard Feather's *The Encyclopedic Yearbook of Jazz* (1956), from the pronunciation of *D.J.,* abbreviation of *disc jockey.* "Tom 'Fly Jock' Joyner . . . , who hosts the *Tom Joyner's Morning Show,* is the nation's most widely syndicated African American deejay" (*Business Week,* July 12, 2004). The word *discotheque* (originally spelled *discothèque*), meaning a club for dancing, especially to recorded music, was borrowed in 1953 from French, in which it was formed on the analogy of *bibliothèque* ("library"). The word was shortened in English to *disco* around 1964. "Discotheque dresses make dancing the frug, the monkey, and the Watusi a delight because they move with the beat" (*TV Guide,* December 12–18, 1964).

Many young people in the '50s took to relaxing social mores and inhibitions, and to espousing various forms of mysticism based on Buddhism and Taoism. They were often tagged the *beat generation.* The name was introduced in an article by John Clellon Holmes in the *New*

York Times of November 16, 1952: "It was the face of the Beat Generation. . . . It was John Kerouac [who said] 'You know, this is really a *beat* generation.'" In *On the Road* (1955–57), Kerouac used *beat* in the sense of "disillusioned, world-weary." But in 1958, J. C. Holmes quoted Kerouac as saying in an interview, "Beat means beatitude, not beat up." The *beat generation* was often shortened to *the beats*, and by 1958 its members came to be known as the *Beatniks*, a coinage by the San Francisco columnist Herb Caen in 1958 from *Beat (generation)* + the suffix *-nik*, influenced by *Sputnik*. In 1959, Kerouac published *The Dharma Bums*, a novel dealing with the beat generation's interest in Zen Buddhism. Fascination with Zen brought into English new terms like *karate, koan* (Zen paradox), and *tai chi chuan* (Chinese martial arts) and popularized older terms like *dharma* (1849, truth), *roshi* (1934, Zen master), and *haiku* (1902, Japanese verse). Introduced from Japanese in 1955, *karate*, meaning literally "empty hand," is a Japanese method of self-defense using hard blows with the hands and feet. A *karate chop* is a fast, sharp blow with the hand. A *karateka* is a karate devotee or expert.

In many ways a literary phenomenon, *beat generation* often referred to a group of U.S. writers that included Jack Kerouac, the poet Allen Ginsberg, and the novelist William Burroughs. But in general, the *Beatniks* formed a counterculture, opposing the conformity and materialism of the 1950s. They were inclined to be unconventional in their attitudes and behavior, dressing casually, the men growing beards and wearing their hair long. Drug use, especially marijuana, was common, due in part to the influence of the books of William Burroughs, especially his novel *Junkie: Confessions of an Unredeemed Drug Addict* (1953), and of Aldous Huxley, whose *The Doors of Perception* (1954) described his hallucinogenic experiences after taking mescaline. The word *hallucinogenic* (1952, "producing hallucinations") was formed from *hallucin*(ation) + *-ogenic*, as in *carcinogenic*. The noun *hallucinogen* for a drug that produces hallucinations was backformed in 1954 from *hallucinogenic*. "Several hallucinogens . . . produce, in addition to other symptoms of schizophrenia, auditory hallucinations" (*New Scientist*, August 28, 1958). The most famous hallucinogen was the drug *LSD*. The term came into English in 1950 as the abbreviation of *Lysergic acid diethylamide*, a powerful drug that produces hallucinations. The abbreviation was actually for its German name of *Lysergsäure-diäthylamid*. "The Beckley Foundation, a British trust, has received approval to begin what will be the first human studies with LSD since the 1970s" (*Time*, April 19, 2007).

A word often used interchangeably with *hallucinogenic* is *psychedelic*, meaning "(of a drug) altering perceptions and sensations by expanding the consciousness and often inducing hallucinations." The word was coined in 1957. A year earlier, in March 1956, the British novelist Aldous Huxley wrote a letter to his friend and neighbor, the psychiatrist Humphry Osmond, proposing the term "phanerothyme" (from Greek *phaneros* "visible" + *thymon* "thyme") for mind-altering agents like mescaline and LSD. "To make this trivial world sublime," rhymed

Huxley, "take half a gramme of phanerothyme." Finding the coinage unpleasant to the ear, Osmond answered Huxley with his own rhyme: "To fathom Hell or soar angelic, Just take a pinch of psychedelic." In 1957, writing in the *Annals of the New York Academy of Science*, Osmond explained his coinage further, using *psychedelic* as an adjective: "I have tried to find an appropriate name for the agents under discussion. . . . My choice, because it is clear, euphonious, and uncontaminated by other associations, is psychedelic, mind-manifesting." The word was a compound of Greek *psychē* "mind, soul" + *dēloun* "to make visible, reveal."

The *beat generation* inspired a parallel term, *Generation X*, which also appeared in 1952, denoting a generation of young people of uncertain future. Originally referring to young Americans of the 1950s, the name came to be applied eventually to the generation following the baby boomers, or those who came of age between 1965 and 1980. It was popularized in the novel *Generation X: Tales of an Accelerated Culture* (1991), by Douglas Coupland. "Generation X may have shed the slacker image over the past decade as its members moved beyond coffee shop jobs and into the suburbs, SUVs and corporate boardrooms" (Jennifer Alsever, *MSNBC News*, November 9, 2007). A member of Generation X is called a *Generation Xer*.

The literary and theatrical world was confounded in the early 1950s with the ascendance of *the Absurd* or *absurdism*, the notion that life and the universe are without meaning. The decade opened with the successful staging of Eugene Ionesco's *The Bald Soprano*, which inaugurated the *Theater of the Absurd* in 1961. It was followed shortly after by Samuel Beckett's acclaimed *Waiting for Godot* (1952). Other significant and influential works of the decade had more to do with fresh views of life than with its presumed absurdity. They included the novels *The Catcher in the Rye* (1951) by J. D. Salinger, Saul Bellow's *The Adventures of Augie March* (1953), and William Golding's *Lord of the Flies* (1954).

The most important development in art during the 1950s was the rise of *abstract expressionism*, a form of painting that emphasized spontaneous or automatic creation. The technique was typified by Jackson Pollock's *action painting*, in which he dripped paint in a seemingly haphazard manner on a large canvas lain on the floor. The intuitive approach of abstract expressionism is believed to have influenced another movement of the '50s, *Pop art* or *pop art*. This form of art used glossy images and artifacts of popular culture, especially advertising and comic books, to create works at once commercial and artistic. Pop art reflected the prosperous mass media of postwar America. The art critic Harold Rosenberg described *Pop art* as "Advertising art which advertises itself as art that hates advertising." Some of the artists associated with Pop art were Jasper Johns, Robert Rauschenberg, Andy Warhol, and Roy Lichtenstein. "Everybody has called Pop art 'American' painting but it's actually industrial painting" (Tilman Osterwold, *Pop Art*, 2003).

Athletics provided the '50s with the *biathlon*, an athletic contest combining two consecutive events, especially a winter sport combining cross-country skiing and precision rifle shooting. The first World Championship in biathlon was held in Austria in 1958, and two years later it was included in the Olympic Games. The word *biathlon* was formed from the combining forms *bi-* "two" + *-athlon*, as in *pentathlon, decathlon* (from Greek *āthlon* "contest"). "The summer biathlons began a few years ago . . . when a handful of Winter Olympics biathlon athletes wanted to have off-season races to help keep in shape" (*New York Times*, July 5, 1989). The *triathlon*, a contest modeled on the biathlon and combining swimming, bicycling, and running, was introduced in 1973.

Important strides in science and technology were made in the 1950s. The most sensational achievement of the decade was the launching by the Soviet Union on October 4, 1957, of the first of a series of *sputniks*, or earth-orbiting artificial satellites.

The first was called *Sputnik 1* and it marked the beginning of the *Space Age* predicted a decade earlier. The word *sputnik* was borrowed from Russian *spútnik* "satellite," literally, "traveling companion," formed from *s* "with" + *pút* "travel, trip," + agent suffix *-nik*. "Fifty years ago . . . the beep-beep-beep of Sputnik was heard round the world" (*New York Times*, September 25, 2007). The term *blast-off*, meaning the launching of a rocket or spacecraft into space, was originally used in the early 1950s in fantasy and science-fiction stories like Martin Greenberg's *Travelers of Space* (1951) and Arthur C. Clarke's *Islands in the Sky* (1952). But after the launching of *Sputnik 1* in 1957, the term blasted off in aerospace usage in 1958. Russian pilots trained to fly spacecrafts were called *cosmonauts* in English starting in 1959. The term was borrowed from Russian *kosmonavt*, from *kosmo-* "world, universe" (from Greek) + *navt* (from Greek *naútēs* "sailor"). "If a cosmonaut's life in orbit or in training is difficult, being a cosmonaut's wife has its own share of problems" (*Space News*, November 3, 2000).

The exploration of outer space introduced earthlings to the age of *aerospace,* the earth's envelope of air and the space beyond. The word *aerospace* first occurred in the phrase *aero space medical research* in 1955. It was soon respelled with a hyphen (*aero-space*), and finally as the solid compound *aerospace.* The word's U.S. spelling did not change to *airspace*, the way *aeroplane* was changed to *airplane*, because *airspace* had already been established since 1908 as meaning the region of the atmosphere directly above an area of land. The form *aero-* is a combining form meaning "of the air or atmosphere," occurring in words like *aerodynamic* and *aeronautics*. The form *aerospace* was first recorded in 1959, in W. A. Heflin's *Aerospace Glossary.*

Delving into theoretical aerospace, astronomers came up in 1950 with the *Big Bang* theory, which is the currently dominant theory of the origin of the universe. The Big Bang was a cosmic explosion that appears to have occurred around thirteen billion years ago, hurling matter through space as it continuously expanded and cooled to form galaxies. Although the first to use the term "big bang"was the British astronomer Fred Hoyle, he referred to it negatively in 1950, when he wrote in *The Listener,*

"This big bang idea seemed to me to be unsatisfactory." The cosmological model Hoyle and others created in 1948, known as the *steady state theory*, is that of a basically static universe, with no beginning or end. But Hoyle was modestly skeptical when he said in an interview, "There is a coherent plan in the universe, though I don't know what it's a plan for."

In earthbound science, no achievement could match the discovery in 1953 of the *double helix*, or helical structure of DNA, by the University of Cambridge team of Francis Crick, James D. Watson, and Rosalind Franklin. Another triumphant first in medicine was the introduction in 1954 of the polio vaccine developed by Jonas Salk. The *Salk vaccine* has helped eradicate the dreaded polio disease from most parts of the world. An important concept in biology introduced in 1959 was that of the *pheromone*, a chemical substance secreted by one member of a species that triggers a specific behavioral response by another member. There are sex pheromones, alarm pheromones, territorial pheromones, and a number of other *pheromonal* substances. The word was formed from Greek *phér* (ein) "to bring" + connective *-o-* + (hor)*mone*. "In most animals, the relationship between pheromones and mating is straightforward. . . . Human pheromones, on the other hand, are highly individualized and not always noticeable" (Deb Levine, CNN, June 25, 1999).

The 1950s ended on an optimistic note with the establishment of the *European Economic Community*, better known as the *Common Market*, and the creation of the U.S. space agency *NASA* (*National Aeronautics and*

Space Administration). The *Hula-Hoop* became a national craze, while the *peace symbol,* a circle incorporating the semaphoric signals for the letters *N* and *D* (for *Nuclear Disarmament*), attained the status of a universal cultural icon. Two other events warmed the hearts of Americans. On January 31, 1958, the United States launched its first earth-orbiting *artificial satellite,* the *Explorer I,* restoring faith in the country's future after its setback by the Soviet Union's launching of *Sputnik I* the previous year. And no less than two new states were added to what came to be known as *the lower 48*: Alaska, on January 3, 1959, and Hawaii, on August 21 of the same year. The 1950s were thus crowned by the fiftieth state of the United States.

Following are some of the notable new words of the 1950s:

academia [1956]. A collective name for the academic world, introduced by William H. Whyte in *The Organization Man* (1956), a study of corporate life in America. Whyte adopted the term from Latin *acadēmia,* the source of English *academy.* "Academia gets creative with Web services" (headline, *CNet News,* October 27, 2003).

ayatollah [1950]. The honorary title of a Shiite religious leader in Iran. The word is first recorded in Donald N. Wilber's book *Iran: Past and Present* (1950). It was a loanword from Persian, from Arabic *āyat allāh* "sign of God." The most famous bearer of the title was Ayatollah Ruholla Khomeini (1902–1989), the Iranian Shiite cleric who returned from exile in 1979 to become the supreme leader of Iran after the departure of the Shah. *Time* magazine spelled the title as *Ayatullah*. "Muqtada Sadr, the Shiite cleric whose supporters are attacking U.S. troops in Iraq, has yet to attain the title of ayatollah" (Brendan Koerner, *Slate*, April 6, 2004).

bonsai [1950]. A dwarfed tree or shrub. The word was from Japanese *bon-sai* "potted plant," which was adopted from Chinese *penjing* "tray planting." "The youngster was in for a treat: Japanese folk dancing, . . . a handmade Japanese doll exhibit, a bonsai tree display" (*Los Angeles Daily News*, July 24, 2005).

colonoscopy [1957]. Examination of the colon by means of a *colonoscope*, a flexible fiberoptic instrument. Both words were first recorded in the 1957 edition of *Dorland's Medical Dictionary* and were formed from *colon* + the combining forms *-scopy* ("viewing") and *-scope* ("instrument for viewing"). "When [Katie] Couric underwent a colonoscopy live on national TV in March 2000, colonoscopy rates nationwide jumped more than 20% in the days and months that followed" (*USA Today*, July 14, 2003).

decaf [1955]. Decaffeinated coffee or tea. This clipped word first appeared in *Nestle's Decaf,* a U.S. trademark, shortened from *decaffeinate* ("to remove coffee from"), a verb used since the 1920s. "Decaf has the same antioxidant benefits as regular coffee" (ABC News, August 28, 2005).

deli [1954]. A short form of *delicatessen* ("delicacies, fine foods"). First recorded in Joseph A. Weingarten's *An American Dictionary of Slang and Colloquial Speech* (1954), with the examples "I'm having deli tonight" and "Mom, let's have deli." The word *delicatessen* came into English from German in the 1880s.

"Dave . . . instructs Rupert to let the . . . deli platter fly down the tub of gravy" (*Late Show with David Letterman,* December 31, 2004).

desegregate [1953]. To eliminate racial segregation. A backformation from earlier (1952) *desegregation,* from the prefix *de-* "undo" + *segregation.* "Court Backs Town's Policy Desegregating Its Schools" (headline, *New York Times,* June 7, 2003).

exurb [1955]. A small community situated beyond the suburbs. Formed from the prefix *ex-* "outside" + (sub)*urb.* The word was coined and popularized by A. C. Spectorsky in his book *The Exurbanites* (1955). In the same book he coined the term *exurbia* as a collective name for the exurbs and the adjective *exurban,* used to describe what he called the *exurbanites.* "Spectorsky does not pretend that all suburbs and exurbs are alike" (*Time,* November 7, 1955).

falafel, felafel [1951]. A dish of small fried balls of chickpeas and spicy salad sandwiched in pita bread. Borrowed (through Hebrew) from Arabic *falāfil.* "The filmmaker's 'West Bank Story', which tells of competing falafel stands in the West Bank, won the live action short film Oscar" (*Los Angeles Daily News,* February 26, 2007).

fall-out [1950]. The radioactive residue of an explosion, especially the explosion of a nuclear bomb. The term first appeared in the government publication *The Effects of Atomic Weapons* (renamed in 1957 *The Effects of Nuclear Weapons*). "So far there have been no dangerous concentrations of radioactive 'fall-out', as it is called, that is outside of the proving grounds in Nevada" (*New York Times,* August 17, 1952).

fast food [1951]. Standardized food prepared and served quickly. First recorded in *Fountain and Fast Food Service* (1951). "In 1970, Americans spent about 66 billion on fast food; in 2000, they spent more than 110 billion" (Eric Schlosser, *Fast Food Nation,* 2001).

film noir [1958]. A motion picture marked by a grim, bleak, pessimistic character. From French, literally, "black film." "A clean print of the lost *film noir* classic *Killers Kill, Dead Men Die* was miraculously discovered at a Mulholland Drive lawn sale last month" (*Vanity Fair,* March 2007).

hi-fi [1950]. High-fidelity equipment. Shortened and altered from *high fidelity* (1934, sound reproduction with little distortion). "The Apple iPod HI-FI ($349 direct) is now part of Apple's steadily growing repertoire of iPod accessories" (*PC magazine,* March 3, 2006).

kiloton [1950]. A unit of explosive force equal to that of a thousand tons of TNT. Formed from *kilo-* "thousand" + *ton.* "The blast from the Hiroshima atomic bomb was 15 kilotons" (*Washington Monthly,* March 1, 2006).

meritocracy [1958]. A system of government or society ruled by people of proven ability and talent rather than wealth, social position, popularity, and the like. When the word *meritocracy* was introduced by the British sociologist Michael Young in *The Rise of the Meritocracy* (1958), it was as a term of contempt. In the book, Young was satirizing a future society whose cult of IQ measurement (and its credo, IQ + Effort = Merit) leads to a smug and arrogant elite that is ultimately overthrown by a revolution of the demoralized masses. Time dealt unkindly with Young's prophecy.

Since the 1950s, *meritocracy* has acquired a positive meaning, probably because the word *merit* has affirmative connotations. The word was formed from *merit* + *-ocracy* "ruling body or class" (as in *aristocracy* or *democracy*). *Meritocracy* shouldn't be confused with a truly negative recent coinage, *mediocracy*, meaning "rule or government by mediocrities."

mom-and-pop, adj. [1951]. Of or pertaining to a small store or shop run by a married couple or family members. First recorded in C. W. Mills's *White Collar: The American Middle Classes.* "Mom-and-pop stores have been a mainstay of the New York City retail scene for generations" (*New York Sun*, August 7, 2007).

nerd [1951]. A dull, foolish, or ineffectual person, especially one obsessively devoted to a technical pursuit, as *a computer nerd.* A U.S. slang word of uncertain origin, perhaps suggested by *Nerd*, a fictional creature in the children's story *If I Ran the Zoo* (1950) by "Dr. Seuss" (Theodor Seuss Geisel). "Unnecessary subplots involving idiotic politicians who act like complete nerds" (*Chicago Sun-Times*, March 29, 1983).

paralegal, adj. [1951]. Of or pertaining to legal assistants or their work. From the prefix *para-* "ancillary, subsidiary" + *legal.* "Mr. Smuts has sent paralegal workers into high schools in five rural and urban areas" (*New York Times*, March 19, 1991).

REM [1957]. The rapidly shifting movements of the eye under closed lids that characterizes the dreaming phase of sleep. Acronym formed from *rapid eye movement.* "Cerebral blood flow . . . has very often been used as a marker of cerebral activity during REM sleep" (B. N. Mallick and S. Inoue, *Rapid Eye Movement Sleep*, 1999).

Scientology [1951]. A system of beliefs and practices founded by the American science-fiction writer L. Ron Hubbard (1911–1986). He first used the term *scientology* in his *Handbook for Preclears* (1951), intended for individuals who receive personal counseling ("auditing") before attaining the stable state of a "Clear." Defining Scientology in 1952 as "the science of knowledge"(from Latin *scient-, scientia* "knowledge" + English *-ology* "study"), Hubbard characterized it as a religion in 1953 and redefined it in 1965 as "an applied religious philosophy dealing with the study of knowledge." The Church of Scientology was established in the same year. Its members are called *Scientologists*: "By watching the fluctuations of a needle, Scientologist 'auditors' can supposedly discern when a student has become 'clear'" (*Time*, August 23, 1968).

Scrabble [1950]. The brand name of a game in which players use tiles displaying individual letters to form words on a playing board. A trademark registered in the U.S. Patent Office, derived from the standard word *scrabble* ("a scrambling or scrawling"). "The game was called 'Lexico' and 'CrissCrosswords' before 'Scrabble' stuck" (*USA Today*, November 5, 2003).

scuba [1952]. A portable device that lets divers breathe underwater. The term is one of the popular acronyms (e.g., *radar*) arising from World War II; the letters stand for *s*elf-*c*ontained *u*nderwater *b*reathing *a*pparatus. In the early 1950s, it was spelled with capital letters (SCUBA); by 1957, it appeared in print in lowercase, the first step of its becoming a standard word. It is often used attributively, as in *scuba diving, scuba equipment*, and in the 1970s, it became a verb, as in *scubaing and swimming in Key Largo*. "Scuba equipment includes, at a minimum, a mask, snorkel, fins . . . instrumentation, and a dive knife" (Dennis Graver, *Scuba Diving*, 2003).

spin-off [1959]. A by-product of something preexisting, as a technological development, a television program, or a new product. A noun compound formed from the verb phrase *spin off* ("to develop or derive [something] from a preexisting thing"). "Fox [Television] is looking to expand its primetime prison population with a spinoff from 'Prison Break'" (*The Hollywood Reporter*, October 24, 2007).

teleprompter [1951]. An off-camera electronic device that displays a magnified script to prompt or assist a speaker. From *TelePrompTer*, a trademark, formed from *tele-* (as in *television*) + *prompter*. "Mr. Obama excels at speeches read from a teleprompter to a mass audience" (*New York Times*, January 13, 2008).

UFO [1953]. An unidentified flying object; a flying saucer. From the abbreviation for *unidentified flying object*. "The Air Force no longer investigates UFOs. . . . Mr. Callanan believes that UFOs are 'possible'" (*Dallas Morning News*, February 3, 2008).

A Selection of New Words of the 1950–1959 Decade

1950

Afro-Asiatic, apparat, appellation contrôlée, aqualung, ayatollah, bar-hopping, bat-mitzvah, berkelium, big bang, bonsai, brainwashing, californium, candela, capsulize (v.), cremains, dianetics, dicey, double-blind, élitism, encrypt (v.), entry level, ergonomics, ethnomusicology, fallout, Gaullism, geekish, hi-fi, information theory, Judenrat, judoist, kiloton,

Klinefelter syndrome, Korean War, lexis, lifemanship, LSD, mano a mano, Maoism, maven, mojo (v.), moonwalker, moving target, multimedia, Munichite, mutagenesis, napalm (v.), ninjutsu, olfactorium, online (adj., adv.), open heart, Orwellian, other-directed, panic button, peace marcher, phonesthesia, polyunsaturate, ponytail, posturepedic, provirus, pupu, ready-mix, recap (n., v.), samba (v.), sanitizer, santeria, scallopini, Scrabble, scram (v.), silvicide, sindonology, smooth-talk (v.), stereophony, stratopause, stressor, Styrofoam, surfactant, tahina, tape-record (v.), telecon, Terramycin, warfarin, work station, zombify, zonk (v.)

1951

Acrilan, baroreceptor, biopic, blast-off, Cinerama, co-occur (v.), cyclamate, Dacron, Day-Glo, demythicize, disconnect (n.), documentarian, drive-by, Eurovision, falafel, fast food, Faulknerian, flambé, graphemic, helidrome, hydrocortisone, institutionalization, knaidel, laundermat, malapportionment, manga, menticide, metalinguist, mom-and-pop, motocross, muon, nanogram, neato, need-to-know, neocolonial, nerd, Nielsen rating, panic button, paralegal, pedophiliac, Pentagonese, pion, pita, plié, psy-war, racy, restructure (v.), role-play (v.), Sarin, showboat (v.), Sonderkommando, sonograph, stapler, stellarator, tailgate (v.), teleprompter, triffid, turbosphere, vacuum-pack, whirlybird, Yinglish

1952

abstract expressionism, achromycin, action painting, Anzus, apolitical, bafflegab, beat generation, cablese, capo, chlorpromazine, Christmas disease, computerized, creepy-peepie, decal, degranulate, desegregation, devein (v.), do-it-yourself, downbeat, downrange, downtime, duplexer, egghead, erythromycin, freeload (n.), grammatology, grosso modo, Interpol, kinesics, lexicostatistic, macroglobulin, McCarthyite, megaton, me-tooer, metrify, mind-bending, monetarize, moonwalk (n.), musique concrète, Mylar, neocolonialism, nightclubber, nitty-gritty, noshery, nuclearist, oligomer, one-upmanship, over-the-transom, pachinko, panelist, photonics, plasmid, pletzel, porn, porno, power-drive (n.), protocontinent, provirus, psephology, radioassay, reserpine, Schweik, scuba, split-level, thunk, triticale, urokinse, vomitous, whomp (v.), wormery, Xerox, wok, Zengakuren

1953

addressable, all-purpose, antimatter, baryon, binit, bleep, bluesman, chlortetracycline, CinemaScope, cladogenesis, cloze, convect (v.), cortisol, countdown, dendroclimatology, desegregate, discotheque, double helix, drip-dry, exolinguistics, exosphere, fly-by, gee (= gravity), glottochronology, governmentese, hippie/hippy, hyperon, hypoallergenic, immunoglobulin, Jet-Ski, kielbasa, klatch, Laetrile, lead-up, maître d', malathion, Medicare, megadeath, microprogram, microvillus, Mitty, monolingualism, monoski, morphospecies, multigene, Murphy's Law, Native Canadian, natriuretic, nerf (v.), nitpicking, ob-gyn, oleh, overfund, overprescribe, paint-by-numbers, palletize, palynologist, parascience, pend (v.), photoresist, piscicide, polyseme, prescriptivism, programmable, Rastafari, shawarma, shoot-'em-up, shootout, sickie, skinhead, smaze, spaghettini, suss (v.), time-sharing, transistorize, UFO, underachiever, videotape, wall-to-wall, water-ski (v.), zonkey

1954

absurdism, aerosoled, air-to-surface, aldosterone, après-ski, automate, barhop (v.), bench-press (v.), bidialectal, bonobo, booboo, bruschetta, capoeirista, cha-cha, codability, coesite, Common Market, contrarian, cosmonaut, cowabunga, Cuisenaire rod, dermabrasion, deli, doo-doo, dragster, ecomorph, extrapolator, FX (= effects), genetic engineer, hallucinogen, juju, kachori, K-meson, Labanotation, lexemic, Lok Sabha, market share, massify, Mickey Mousing, micrometeroid, microsite, mid-teen, Miltown, misalign, mondegreen, moped, Mossad, multipartism, multitrack, myxovirus, nanny (v.), narco, oceanologist, offroad, off-target, old media, Ondes Martentot, oxymoronic, pally-wally, parasexual, pasties, pay TV, photoactivate, piezzoresistance, pizzetta, polyomino, prioritize, protostar, pugil stick, rock 'n' roll, Salk vaccine, Sapir-Whorf hypothesis, SEATO (Southeast Asia Treaty Organization), segregationist, sequence (v.), serotype, shush, Spansule, stereo, supermart, Thorazine, torque (v.), urbiculture, Vistavision

---

1955

admass, aerospace, agoraphobe, agribusiness, A-line, alphanumeric, autopista, Baath, badass, bazoom, benny (= benzedrine), boogie (v.), cohabitee, counterintuitive, decaf, disinformation, doo-wop, eat-in, ECHO virus, eigenfrequency, einsteinium, exurb, exurbia, fedayeen, fermium, hot list, hummus, inner child, integrationist, ionsonde, karate, Katyusha, lingonberry, lite, live-in, lysosome, maser, mendelevium, micromachining, mind-boggling, monkey bars, muonic, neo-expressionist, New Left, nine-to-fiver, noctambulate, nonleaded, nouveau, oomphy, packrat (v.), Panavision, Parkinson's Law, pétanque, philobat, phytotoxicant, pinball (v.), pitch-up, poppit bead, postcolonialism, Poujadism, preamp, prednisone, prefab (v.), proette, promo, quick smart (adv.), Rasta, Rastafarian, roll-on roll-off, Sabin vaccine, schiz, sci-fi, seaquarium, snowcat, sonics, spacelab, space launcher, spinto, sterliant, subtopia, surfer, tabbouleh, texting (music), therapize,

Tobagonian, Travolator, valinomycin, vegie, vodkatini, voyeurist, weirdo, wire-tap (n.), yipes, zinger

---

1956

abs (muscles), academia, adenovirus, aikido, alphameric, base pair, birdie (v.), botel, buzkashi, cryotron, deejay, Dom Pérignon, ecdysone, Euratom, Fortran (programming language), free-fall (v.), glitterati, hinky, Hugo, hypercharge, Indy, in-house, jumboize, limbo (dance), long-running, margherita, materials science, medfly, metalaw, middle earth, Miesian, minitrack, mogul (skiing), Moho, Nasserism, navaid, nidality, 1984, nitpick (v.), nuclearize, Obie, oopsy, origami, pachanga, particle board, patch-test (v.), phonotactic, photoscan, plasmoid, pleasuredome, polyribonucleotide, proact (v.), problem-solve (v.), promazine, psychomimetic, psychotropic, radiolabel (v.), ranchette, retardate, retrofit, rockabilly, Rube Goldberg, Scotchgard, segmentalize, sonogram, specs, squaresville, squop (v.), streptomycete, tech (adj.), trad (n.), Tupperware, uke, underwhelm, vancomycin, weaponized, zircalloy

---

1957

ahistorical, arborvirus, backgrounder, barfy, bleep (v.), cheongsam, Chinglish, cistron, cite (n.), colonoscope, colonoscopy, computer scientist, endsville, enterovirus,

ethnolinguist, eukaryon, free-range (v.), Frisbee, halothane,
hoisin (sauce), the Holocaust, insensitivity, interferon,
interrupt (n.), kente, koan, kuru, Lego, mammoplasty,
marine scientist, Metro (adj.), megabit, mercy-kill (v.),
micrometer, microprogram, Minamata disease,
minimax (v.), minty, mitogenesis, moisturizer, moonshot,
mountainscape, multiculturalism, multiracialism,
multiversity, muonium, Muzak (v.), mycophobic, narcolept,
natriuresis, neo-expressionism, NORAD (North American
Air Defense Command), off-off Broadway, opioid, orthotics,
ostomy, overkill (n.), Parkinsonism, photoisomer, pionic,
play-Doh, Polaris (missile), poopy, Pop art, pothead, potty
(v.), preamp, premix, prêt-à-porter, prokaryon, psychedelic,
psychogeriatric, Pugwash, pyroceram, quasiparticle,
radiolabel (n.), RAM (random-access memory), REM,
RNase, role-play (n.), son et lumière, spaceshot, spaz (v.),
sputnik, summiteer, tellurometer, transsexual, Viet Cong,
weaponize, wedeln, whiplash (v.), writerly

1958

agrichemical, amniocentesis, angiotensin, archeometry,
artificial satellite, audiotape, bad-talk (v.), Beatnik, biathlon,
bluesy, bootstrap (v.), chromatograph, computerization,
containerize, data set, film noir, fladge, hot-link, Hula
Hoop, in-box, kaon, klepto, lo-fi, loid, Lycra, mai tai,

mammogenesis, mass spectroscope, melatonin, mesc, microcode, microminiature, Mittyesque, modem, mucositis, multievent, mythogenic, nanosecond, NASA (National Aeronautics and Space Administration), neuroleptic, nuke, on-board, orbiter, Oscar (v.), paralinguistics, peace symbol, pentatonicism, people-watching, phase-out, photoset, pick 'n' mix, planeful, polymerase, polyoma, preactivate, prequel, pretape (v.), psilocybin, quads (muscles), rhubarb (v.), recusal, ribosome, Rolf (massage), sched, scintillogram, self-medicate, send-up, sensor, serendipitous, situationist, Skinnerian, soft landing, sonicate, souvlaki, Sovietology, stereophonics, summitry, suppressant, tandoori, thalidomide, unflappable, victimology, Viet, visagiste

1959

academese, actorly, Algol (programming language), Barbie, balls-out, beat poet(ry), binge eating, boo, campy, CB radio, chad, charbroil (v.), circadian, clone (v.), codswallop, colorectal, computer science, co-pay (n.), cosmonaut, counterproductive, country-and-western (music), dopamine, down-and-dirty, dreamscape, Efta (European Free Trade Association), ekistics, electronic mail, Euramerican, fantabulous, Fidelism, floatel, go-kart, Grammy, hash, hovercraft, immunoglobulin, innumeracy (-ate), isozyme, kooky, Lamaze, lepidoptery, logophile, Lolita, macro,

magnetosphere, mass-market (v.), match-up,
microcircuit(ry), microelectronics, microminiaturize,
modacrylic, monstre sacré, motelier, multiprogramming,
muscledom, Nabokovian, Nardil, neatnik, neocolonialist,
nouveau roman, nouvelle vague, Nowheresville, numeracy
(-ate), nutcase, OD (= overdose), off-off-off-Broadway,
ofuro, omnicide, one-upman, optoelectronics, pantyhose,
personal computer, phenotype (v.), pheromone,
photoscanner, planification, plugola, powerlifting, prefab
(v.), privatization, programmable, (computer) programming
language, pseudocide, psychoactive, reovirus, reusable,
rifamycin, rotavate, saketini, schussboomer, Seyfert (galaxy),
sheesh (interj.), shrink-wrapping, Spandex, spin-off, stir-fry,
supremacist, Tantricism, tensegrity, teratogen, tetrathlon,
ufology, Uzi, Van Allen (belt), vexillology, virion,
washeteria, Wicca, zendo, zonked

Chapter 7

The Turbulent Sixties:

1960–1969

The 1960s were years of social unrest and turmoil that thoroughly transformed American society. Yet the decade began on an optimistic note. In the words of Joan and Robert K. Morrison, authors of an anthology about the 1960s, *From Camelot to Kent State* (1987): "The Decade started, hopefully enough, with the election of John F. Kennedy to the presidency. At his inauguration he called upon Americans to 'ask not what your country can do for you, ask rather what you can do for your country.' . . . We were going to go to the moon. We were going to end poverty. The arts would flourish." That time and place of glamorous doings was to be widely and romantically known as *Camelot,* an allusion to King Arthur's court. Young people flocked idealistically to join the *Peace Corps,* which was established in 1961, or *VISTA (Volunteers in Service to America),* the 1964 domestic counterpart of the Peace Corps, or to play a part in President Kennedy's domestic and international program, promisingly called the *New Frontier.*

Setbacks began early in the decade. As the Cold War intensified, President Kennedy sent fifteen thousand military "advisers" to South Vietnam, the prelude to American involvement in the *Vietnam War,* which would last till 1975. The long war produced a new vocabulary: *Nam*

(= Vietnam), *Viet* (= Vietnamese), *Vietcong* (enemy guer-
rilla force, nicknamed *Victor Charlie* or *Charlie* or *VC*), *Vietnik* (an antiwar protester, synonymous with *peacenik*), *grunt*
(a U.S. soldier or marine), *Vietnamization, body count* (a
count of the enemy killed in combat), *kill ratio* (the propor-
tion of casualties on either side in combat), *gook, dink, slope*
(all slang terms for a Vietnamese), the *Tet Offensive* (a 1968
surprise attack by the Viet Cong), and the *My Lai massacre*
(of the inhabitants of a South Vietnamese village in 1968).

Meanwhile, the Cold War took the form of the *space
race,* the competition between the United States and
the U.S.S.R. to be the first to explore outer space. The
Soviet Union won an initial victory when on April 12,
1961, the *cosmonaut* Yuri Gagarin became the first human
to travel in outer space and to orbit the earth (for 108 minutes). Eight years later the United States won the race to
put a man on the moon in the *Apollo* program, when on
July 20, 1969, the *Apollo 11* astronauts Neil Armstrong and
Buzz Aldrin Jr. became the first humans to walk on the
moon. The *space age* introduced into the language many
new terms preceded by *"space"*—such as *space capsule,
spacelab, spaceshot, space shuttle, spacesuit, spacewalk*—as
well as novel space-age terms like *hard lander* and *soft
lander, reentry* and *splashdown, command module, service
module, lunar rover, lunarnaut,* and *lunarscape.*

A famous space-age coinage, *A-OK* or *A-okay,*
meaning "All is well, everything is functioning perfectly,"
surfaced in 1961. It was supposed to be an exclamation
used by astronauts after a successful mission, as an
abbreviation of *All (systems) OK.* In the book *First on the*

Moon (1970), by Neil Armstrong, Michael Collins, and Edwin "Buzz" Aldrin Jr., the authors claim that the phrase was never used by astronauts but was coined by a public relations officer. Still, the legend persists that Alan Shepard, the first U.S. astronaut, used it while returning from space on the *Freedom 7* spacecraft on May 5, 1961.

In the 1960s, the Cold War divided the world into three economic and ideological parts. One part was the *Third World* (1963), comprising the group of underdeveloped countries, especially of Africa and Asia (originally, countries not aligned with either the Communist or the non-Communist world). "The students, following the gospel of [Herbert] Marcuse, look to the Third World, to Fidel Castro, and Ho Chi Minh, for salvation" (*New York Times Magazine*, April 28, 1968). The term is a translation of French *Tiers Monde,* recorded since 1956. The derivatives *Third Worlder* and *Third Worldism* (support for the Third World) appeared in 1970. Another part was the *Second World* (1967), comprising the Communist or socialist countries of the world. The last was the *First World* (1967), the major industrialized countries of the world, including the United States, western Europe, Japan, and the Soviet Union. In the 1970s, a *Fourth World* was added to the mix, consisting of the poorest, most marginalized, and usually stateless peoples of the world. "Arab producers may be pressed to 'invest' in a development bank—where they probably will practice 'neocolonialism' on their poorer brothers, who are now called the Fourth World" (*Harper's*, June 1974).

In the United States, a major issue in the early '60s

was the struggle of African Americans in the South to obtain civil rights, which included organizing bus boycotts against racial segregation on buses, *sit-ins* (a word first applied to striking workers in 1937) at segregated lunch counters, and a slew of other *-ins* (e.g., *eat-ins, kneel-ins, lie-ins, shop-ins, stand-ins, swim-ins*). Their efforts paid off when the government took notice and introduced the policy and program of *affirmative action* in 1961 to compensate for past discrimination in employment, education, and housing by increasing opportunities in these areas for African Americans and other minorities. The term originated in a series of presidential directives, as this one from Executive Order 11246, 1965: "The contractor will take affirmative action to ensure that applicants are employed . . . without regard to their race, creed, color, or national origin." Some of the civil-rights tactics were used by antiwar groups as the United States sank deeper into the Vietnam War, their protests including sit-ins as well as *talk-ins, teach-ins,* and *study-ins* (by university teachers and students).

The civil-rights struggle in America inspired a growing opposition to all kinds of discriminatory practices, especially against minorities. A primary focus was discrimination or prejudice based on a person's sex, which gave rise to the term *sexism* in 1968. Though the term was used mainly in reference to discrimination by men against women, it was sometimes applied to female prejudices against males, as well as to prejudices by both genders against transsexuals, gays, and so on. The defining event of the gay rights movement was the outbreak of the *Stonewall* riots on June 28, 1969, at the Stonewall Inn in New York's Greenwich

Village, in which a group of homosexuals rebelled against their state-sponsored persecution. The word *sexism* was formed on the model of *racism* (1933), though it was clearly influenced by the earlier (1961) adjective *sexist*. "*Sexism*, like *racism* and *feminism*, and some other *isms* too, is a much-vexed and tormented term today" (Kenneth G. Wilson, *The Columbia Guide to Standard American English*, 1993). A year after the coinage of *sexism*, an American gerontologist, Robert N. Butler, coined the term *ageism* to denote discrimination or prejudice against people of a certain age, especially older people. The adjective *ageist*, paralleling *sexist*, appeared in 1970. These words formed a pattern for similar coinages in the 1970s, such as *heightism* (1971, discrimination against short people), *lookism* (1978, discrimination based on people's looks), and *ableism* (1981, discrimination against the disabled).

A radical movement of the times was the *hippie* counterculture, which flourished in the mid-1960s. *Hippies* were usually young people who dressed unconventionally as *street people* and maintained a philosophy of love and fellowship, often living in *communes* and engaging in free love. They frequently wore flowers on their hair or handed out flowers (earning the epithet *flower children* or *flower people*), and freely used drugs like cannabis (*pot, grass, maryjane*) and hallucinogens (*LSD* or *acid, psilocybin, mesc* for mescaline, *hash* for hashish). The hippie movement spawned a special vocabulary: *acidhead* (LSD user), *acid rock* (type of rock 'n' roll), *acid trip, bad trip, bummer, dashiki* (loose, brightly colored shirt), *head shop* (selling psychedelic artifacts), *heat* (= police), *mind-blowing, mind-*

expanding (both meaning *psychedelic*), *yippies* (politically active hippies). Emulating the *sit-ins* of social and political protesters, hippies staged *love-ins, smoke-ins*, and *be-ins* (at which participants *did their own thing*). The hippie revolution culminated in *Woodstock*, a legendary rock-music festival held on a farm in the town of Bethel, New York, on which nearly four hundred thousand hippies or hippie sympathizers converged on August 15–18, 1969, in a monumental *happening*. *Hippie* meant originally (1952) "a person who is overly *hip* (eager to be ahead in the latest styles), a *hipster*." The word's meaning was extended in 1966–67 through the widespread publicity given in the media to the drug scene in New York and San Francisco. "A few wear the garb of hippies—beards, beads, jeans, long gowns" (*New York Times*, August 6, 1968).

An expression uniquely associated with the hippie counterculture is *turn on, tune in, drop out.* The expression was coined and popularized by the American psychologist Dr. Timothy Leary (1920–1996), who became a controversial figure in the '60s for experimenting with and advocating the use of psychedelic drugs like LSD and psilocybin. Leary first used the three-phrase expression in a speech he made in 1967 at the "Human Be-In," a large gathering of hippies in San Francisco. He said that the three short phrases occurred to him after the Canadian communications theorist Marshall McLuhan suggested that he should come up with a snappy slogan to promote the benefits of using psychedelic drugs. Leary used the expression as the title of book of essays that is still in print. In his autobiography, *Flashbacks* (1983), he explained the meaning of the slogan: " 'Turn on' meant go within to . . . become sensitive to the many and various levels of consciousness and the specific triggers that engage them. Drugs were one way to accomplish this end. 'Tune in' meant interact harmoniously with the world around you. . . . 'Drop out' meant self-reliance, a discovery of one's singularity, a commitment to mobility, choice, and change. Unhappily my explanations of this sequence of personal development were often misinterpreted to mean 'Get stoned and abandon all constructive activity.' "

Influenced by the freedom of expression emanating from the hippie subculture, many young fans of rock-music stars joined forces as *teeny-boppers* and *groupies* to flock to the concerts of their idols, who flooded the airwaves with combinations like *folk rock* and *raga rock*. Another musical phenomenon was the spread of *discos* (short for *discotheques*), where *go-go girls* undulated to the latest dance fads, such as the *frug*, the *Watusi*, the *ska*, wild dances in which the partners didn't touch or talk, and the *bossa nova*, a Brazilian dance related to the samba. The arrival in the United States of the Beatles, a Liverpool rock and pop group, created a craze promptly dubbed *Beatlemania*, which lasted till the end of the decade and made the group the most popular *rockers* in history.

In the art world, *neo-Dadaism* or *neo-Dada*, a contemporary development of the anti-art theories and techniques of Dadaism, emerged in the early '60s as the work of a group of *neo-Dadaists* that include artists like Robert Rauschenberg, Jasper Johns, Yves Klein, and Nam June Paik. Another art form, *optical art*, better known as *Op art* (after *Pop art*), became prominent in the mid-1960s. *Op art* is a form of abstract art that makes use of optical illusions and other optical effects and is associated with *op artists* (or *optical artists*) like Bridget Riley, Victor Vasarely, Josef Levi, and Richard Allen.

In the world of fashion, hemlines were all the rage of the '60s. The four M's of fashion were the *maxi, micro, midi,* and *mini.* "In their desperation to whet consumer demand by the good, old American economic device of forced obsolescence," wrote Marilyn Bender in the *New York Times* of July 5, 1968, "the [fashion] industry's merchants, manufacturers, and editors have been touting the midi, the maxi and other varieties of lowered hemlines." Through a good part of the '60s, women's hemlines went to extremes. Skirts, dresses, coats, and other garments could reach to the ankle or just above it (*maxis* or *maxiskirts, maxidresses,* etc.), or end two to four inches above the knee (*minis* or *miniskirts,* etc.), or be even shorter than the minis, barely covering the backside (*micros* or *microskirts,* etc.), or could find a happy medium in the *midis,* which reached to the midcalf. Some thought that these styles reflected the uncertainty of the times; others thought that they were a rejection by the youth culture of old-fashioned grace, elegance, and good taste.

In technology, the development in the late 1950s and early 1960s of programming languages for computers, such as *Algol, Basic, Cobol,* and *Fortran,* made possible the *software* required for the operation of computers. The newly emerging *computer science* (1959) spurred during the 1960s the coinage of a host of new technical and semitechnical terms such as *byte, megabyte, cursor, database, GIGO, microchip, mouse, read-only memory (ROM),* and *random-access memory (RAM).* The widespread use of computers popularized the combining form *cyber-* to form words dealing with computers and information technology, among them *cyberculture* (the culture of computer use) and *cyberspace,* and nonce coinages like *cyberphobia, cybernocracy,* and *cyberworld.*

In medicine, the '60s heralded the forthcoming sexual revolution with the introduction of *the Pill* (oral contraceptive for women) for general use in the United States, while the first *in vitro fertilization* of human egg cells was achieved in Cambridge, England. At the same time, the drug *thalidomide,* long used as a sedative by pregnant women, was banned after it was shown to cause congenital malformations in newborn babies. In 1967, Dr. Christiaan Barnard, a South African surgeon, performed the first successful *heart transplant,* and screening *mammograms* was shown to save breast cancer victims. To advance the nation's health system, President Lyndon B. Johnson's *Great Society* program introduced in 1965–1966 *Medicare* and *Medicaid* for the elderly and the poor.

The decade also saw the establishment of *OPEC* (Organization of Petroleum-Exporting Countries), the oil cartel that triggered a worldwide crisis in oil prices in 1973. On the positive side, the nuclear-weapon *Non-Proliferation Treaty* was signed by sixty-one nations. Technological advances in the '60s included the demonstration of the first working *laser* (for generating or amplifying a beam of light), and the launching of *Telstar,* the first active *communications satellite (comsat)*, able to transmit live television pictures. In 1963, the U.S. Post Office introduced the *Zip Code* (originally *ZIP*, for Zone Improvement Plan), a system of codes used to identify mail-delivery zones; and in 1968, the *911* emergency telephone system was established in the United States.

Gradually the chaotic '60s wound down, and Americans began to turn from antiwar activism and countercultural radicalism to self-interest and self-improvement. This trend had many facets, from encounter groups and sensitivity-training groups to Oriental religious groups and ESP psychic groups and Jesus People. These became known as *Me* movements, and the entire generation as the *Me Generation*. While the '60s were all about *Them*, the '70s were all about *Me*.

Here are some notable new words of the 1960s:

aerobics [1968]. A system of developing physical fitness by correlating oxygen consumption and pulse rate with exercises like running, walking, swimming, and dancing. The system was popularized by Kenneth H. Cooper, a U.S. Air Force physiologist, in his book *Aerobics* (1968). *Aerobic* exercises are contrasted with *anaerobic* ones, which are of short duration and are designed to build muscle mass. The term *aerobic* derives from *aero-* "air" + (micr)*obe*, an organism that can live in the presence of oxygen.

black hole [1968]. A region in space into which stars and other celestial objects collapse under the influence of gravity. "The 'black holes' predicted by the general theory of relativity [are] objects so compact that even light cannot escape their gravitational pull. The black hole is the destiny of all stars whose terminal mass considerably exceeds the mass of the sun" (*Scientific American*, February 1971).

born-again [1961]. Characterized by a renewed commitment to Christ as the way to salvation. The adjective is often synonymous with *evangelical*, as in *a born-again Baptist, the born-again fundamentalist movement.* The phrase became widely known in the 1970s, after presidential candidate Jimmy Carter described himself as "a born-again Christian." The source of the phrase is the Gospel of John (3:3): "Jesus answered and said unto him, Verily, verily, I say unto thee, Except a man be born again, he cannot see the kingdom of God."

nuke, v. [1962]. To destroy or attack with nuclear weapons. A verb use of the noun *nuke* (1958), meaning "a nuclear weapon," shortened and altered from *nuclear.* The verb's use was extended in 1967 to the figurative meaning "to destroy, exterminate, or ruin" and narrowed in college campus slang in 1984 to "to cook or heat in a microwave oven, to microwave."

paparazzo (pl. paparazzi or paparazzos) [1961]. An aggressive freelance photographer who pursues celebrities to take their pictures for sale to tabloids and other publications. "They are the *paparazzi* of the London picture market, a wheeling horde of newly self-styled impresarios of the arts" (*London Sunday Times,* April 13, 1969). The word was borrowed from Italian, after *Paparazzo,* the name of a society photographer in Federico Fellini's film *La Dolce Vita* (1960). According to the *Oxford English Dictionary,* the selection of the name of the character in the film has been explained variously, one explanation being a comment attributed to Fellini that the name "suggests a buzzing insect, hovering, darting, stinging."

pulsar [1968]. A rapidly rotating neutron star that emits pulses of radiation with a high degree of regularity. The first pulsar was discovered in 1967 and named by contraction of *puls*(ating st)*ar*, on the model of *quasar*.

quark [1964]. Any of a group of subatomic particles that never occur in a free state, have a fractional electric charge, and are thought to be basic constituents of matter. The six known types of quarks, called *flavors*, are the *down quark, up quark, charmed quark, bottom quark, top quark*, and *strange quark*. The antiparticle of a quark is an *antiquark*. The word was coined by the U.S. physicist Murray Gell-Mann, who thought that all matter consists of three basic building blocks, which he called *quarks*, from the line "Three quarks for Muster Mark!" in James Joyce's *Finnegans Wake*.

quasar [1964]. A celestial object originally thought to be a *quasi-stellar* radio source but now thought to be the extremely bright center of a distant galaxy whose energy is due to the presence of a supermassive black hole at its center. The word is a contraction of *qua*(si)-*s*(tell)*ar*. "The puzzling quasars are believed to be less than 10 light-years in diameter—compared with the 100,000-light-year diameter of a typical galaxy—yet they are pouring out 100 times more light than a typical galaxy of 100 billion stars" (*1969 Collier's Encyclopedia Yearbook*).

unisex [1968]. Not distinguishing between the sexes; designed or suitable for either a male or female. "Greenwich Village, always the firstest with the weirdest, has just spawned the world's 'first unisex boutique for men and women from 16 to 25' " (*Manchester Guardian Weekly*, November 21, 1968). The word was formed from *uni-* "one" + *sex*, and produced the derivatives *unisexed, unisexual*, and *unisexuality*. "In ballet, adults adore the unisexuality of Nureyev" (*Time*, October 12, 1970).

A Selection of New Words of the 1960–1969 Decade

1960

ABD (All But Dissertation), arugula, barf (v.), bionics, biorhthym, body art, bookmark (v.), breakout (adj.), breathalyzer, bricolage, Castroism, cliometrics, Cobol, commute (n.), computerese, computerize, contractee, crudités, C-section, cyborg, daytimer, deboard (v.), découpage, deke (ice hockey), derepress (v.), despin (v.), dreadlocks, dullsville, dumbo, edit (n.), eldercare, encryption, ephemeralization, exploitability, feeding frenzy, freeze-frame, gran turismo, Hezbollah, home shopping, homophile, implantable, indexation, jamas (= pajamas), Japlish, kidult, kineticist, kneel-in, kook, laser, lawned, leopon, Librium, machine-wash (v.), mae-geri (karate), mag tape, market-test (v.), meritocrat, metafiction, metatheater, minicab, minivan, missileer, mix-and-match (adj.), namaste, nerdy, New Leftist, new media, no-frill (adj.), noodge (v.), nuclearization, off-camera, paperback (v.), paraprofessional, PG (= pregnant), photojournalistic, pop-cult, pre-teen, pro-life (adj.), promo (v.), run-and-gun (adj.), scarf (= eat), screw-up, snarl-up, soft-land (v.), software, space age, surveil (v.), trend-setter, upchuck (v.), Velcro, wade-in, wheeler-dealer

1961

acidy, actorish, admix, advertorial, affirmative action,
Afghanistanism, aleatoric (music), all-you-can-eat (adj., n.),
Amex, ao dai (Vietnamese garment), A-OK, attendee,
back-talk (v.), bio, born-again, bratty, descriptivism, dial-up
(n., adj.), dishy, docudrama, dolce vita, doomsayer, Down's
syndrome, draft-dodger, ecumenics, Elint, endistance (v.),
Eurocrat, fab (= fabulous), favela, gerontocrat, gillion (1,000
million), grammaticality, grok (v.), identikit, keyboard (v.),
kidnap (n.), lifeway, line dance, linerboard, make-ahead
(adj.), malapportioned, mascara (v.), memo (v.), microwave
(v.), moon shot, mooseburger, multiprocessor, neo-Dada,
nitpicking (adj.), no-hope (adj.), no-win (adj.), nymphette,
ombudswoman, omigod, packageable, pair-bonding,
paparazzo, paraglider, perfecta, permissivism, pied noir,
porny, power broker, psyched, reentry (of spacecraft),
read-in, reprography, ROM (read-only memory), Sangria,
schmeer, service module, sexist, shtik, Skidoo, skyjack (v.),
sleep-in (adj.), soft lander (spacecraft), splashdown,
spritzer, stat (= statistic), study-in, swim-in, Synanon,
ton-up (= 100 mph), trade-off, unitard, Valium, vid
(= video), Vietcong, walk-in, wazoo, wedeln (v.), wheel
and deal, zazzy

1962

access (v.), auteur, bait and switch, bilayer, bossa nova, comsat, cybernation, database, de-orbit (v.), digitalize, drop-dead (adj.), expat (= expatriate), filmography, glitch (n., v.), go-go (adj.), gremmie (surfing), happening (public performance), hard lander (spacecraft), head-counter, hodad (surfing), joual, kludge, lase (v.), leaflet (v.), Madison (group dance), mao-tai, micro-oven, minibike, mixed media, multimedia, Nam, no-hit (v.), non-proliferation, nuke (v.), oceanaut, paper-clip (v.), parallel parking, Pekingology, pesty, plantsmanship, porn, pre-med, pseudo-event, psilocybin, repo, retro-fire (n.), slow-dance (v.), slurb, spacesuit, spacewoman, splittism, surfie, teriyaki, ticky-tacky, tokenism, trendy, turn-on, tush, ujamaa, upmanship, voiceprint, Wasp, with-it (adj.), win-win, yakitori

---

1963

aggiornamento, answerphone, antilock, appraisee, après-skiing, ASCII (computer code), Beatle, benchmark (v.), cinéma vérité, cinephile, codon, computer graphics, Cosa Nostra, cyberculture, cybercultural, decriminalize, degradable, demystify, deregulation, dialogue de sourds (= dialogue of the deaf), diddly-squat, disambiguate (v.), ecumaniac, euphemics, Expo, free-marketeer, funkster, Hawthorne effect, herbivory, home-schooling (adj.), immunosuppression, jargonaut, lidar, lie-in, machine-washable, mail-in, Mickey Mouse (v.), microcomputer, mind-expanding, mind game, mini (adj.), monoski, nannydom, neo-Pentecostalism, neuroscience, old money, peacenik, phat (adj.), Pinyin, plea bargain, popster, RAM (random-access memory), ryokan, scam (n., v.), single-blind (adj.), snarf (v.), sociologese, space capsule, spacewalk, supercontinent, telecom, Third World, treff (n.), ucky, uomo universale, videogram, Vietnam War, Water Pik

---

1964

aerosol (v.), antiquark, A-team, bariatrics, BASIC (computer language), bleeper, byte, choreology, computerist, computerology, command module, condo, de-escalation, demythify, denturist, disco, dork, ecofact, ecozone, ephebophile, ephebophilia, equitability, ethnonym, exacta, fish-in, format (v.), Franglais, GIGO (= garbage in, garbage out), grotty, heimish, immunosuppressant, in-joke, kidology, kippah, kvetch, mack daddy, macroeconomist, Marlboro Country, marv (= marvelous), Metabolist, microlens, microteaching, mininess, mono (= mononucleosis), monokini, multiaccess, nad (= gonad), naloxone, namesmanship, nanovolt, neuroscientist, ninja, nitpicky, olfactronics, ooky, op art, quark, quasar, rat fink, raunch, schlub, schmegeggy, sitcom, ska, skank, skateboard, suicidology, triumphalism, TV land, vox-pop, yakuza, yuck it up, Zambian, zeitgeber

1 9 6 5

à gogo, Air Cav, Amerasian (adj.), audio-animatronics, autocross, bachelorette, bada-bing (interj.), basilect, boogaloo, bricoleur, chartbuster, clunky, computer-graphic (adj.), computeritis, computery (adj.), consumerist, cryonics, cryopreservation, culturati, cybernaut, digitalization, dooky, eat-in, escalatory, Eurocentrism, foodaholic, free fire zone, gang-bang (v.), Godzilla, go-see (n.), graphicacy, grody, grunge, grungy, hone in, hypermedia, hypertext, keiretsu, lunarnaut, lunarscape, Medicare, megabyte, mentee, metricate, metrication, metrification, middlescence, middlescent, minidress, miniskirt, moby, mockumentary, motorcade (v.), Motown, (computer) mouse, Murphy (v.), OD (= overdose, v.), oracy, overclass, parajournalism, peacenik, pedway, pick-list, policeperson, proactivity, psy-op, pyramid selling, sexist, shop-in, spacescape, spacewalking, spaz, stagflation, stand-in, teach-in, victimless crime, Vietnik, Zamboni, zine

1 9 6 6

acid (LSD), acidhead, acid rock, aerophobe, aliterate, Amerasian, Art Deco, as-told-to (adj.), Astroturf, AWACS (Airborne Warning and Control System), bad trip, barf (n.), Chicom, cinematheque, computernik, co-payment, crystal meth, cyber-, defogger, Denticare, Dolby, dunk (n.), flack (v.), folkie, foosball, glitzy, grinch, gross-out, guitary, headcase,

hippie, house-sitter, incendijell, Jacuzzi, jams, karate (v.),
kung-fu, Mace (v.), medevac, Medicaid, meth
(= methamphetamine), meth freak, meth head, mind-
blowing, mini, mondo (bizarro), multitasking, mwah, narc
(n.), ngwee, number cruncher, olfactronic, ombudsmanship,
parajournalist, paramedic, personal computing,
plasmasphere, ponzu sauce, primavera (adj.),
psychedelicatessen, pschedelicize, Quaalude, quanton,
radio-tag (v.), ralph (v.), self-destruct (v.), Shirley Temple
(drink), skinny-dip (v.), soul-search (v.), spacewalk (v.),
talk-in, teeny-bopper, tempeh, trendiness, upscale (adj.),
urbicide, VAT (value added tax), wakeboard, wheelie,
whiteboard, xerox (v.), yada-yada, yuck (interj.), zilch, zit

1967

acid trip, Afrocentric, amp (= amplifier), balls-to-the-wall
(adj.), be-in, Biafran, blivit, body artist, breathalyze (v.),
Botswanan, bummer, cheapo, (hippie) commune,
computerphile, crêperie, cruiseway, cursor, Dancercize,
decollate (v.), deinstitutionalization, Denver shoe, depollute
(v.), doobie, doofus (adj., n.), downrate, downwell, el cheapo,
evapotranspire, faction (fact + fiction), flower children,
flower people, fry-up, gofer, gomer, hash (= hashish), head
shop (psychedelic store), heat (= police), Hinglish, hoagie,
honky, ibuprofen, informatics, jihadist, klick (= kilometer),

kurchatovium, kvell (v.), litterfall, love-in, mailout, maxi, McLuhanism, merc (= mercenary), micro-mini, mike (= microgram), mill-in, minicomputer, minigolf, Miranda (warning), MIRV (missile), monetarism, monetarization, monohull, Moog synthesizer, multipack, multiscreen, Nehru jacket, no-fault (adj.), no-frills (adj.), noodge (v.), omega-3, outro, paint-spray (v.), peer review, people-watch (v.), Peter principle, phone-in, RV (recreational vehicle), samizdat, shiatsu, slimnastics, space race, Spanglish, street people, tae kwon do, urbanology, Viet, vroom

1968

aerobics, artsy, auteurism, bippy, Black English, black hole, blindside (v.), body count, cellulite, computerspeak, coronavirus, cutesy, educrat, firmware, FOB (Fresh Off the Boat), Fosbury Flop, Ginnie Mae, goombah, Hare Krishna, holograph (v.), house-sitting, incentivize, incrementalism, kill ratio, kleptocrat, Klingon, laugh-in, limo, low riding, Mace (v.), mail-order (v.), mammograph, Marsquake, mascon (= mass concentration), megavitamin, micro, midi, minikini, minipill, MIRV (v.), mondo (adj.), multitask (adj.), NASDAQ, 911 (emergency phone number), nitpick (n.), noodge (n.), novela, number crunching, om (v.), omigosh (interj.), out-of-body (adj.), pager, peekapoo (dog breed), pizza face, psychotronic, psychotronics, pube, pulsar, reggae, rurp, SALT (Strategic Arms Limitation Talks), scuzz, scuzzy, sexism, skyjack (v.), smoke-in, (Dr.) Strangelove, sudser, toke (n.), tsatske, tchotchke, unisex (adj., n.), vibe (v.), Waspish, Waspy, workaholic, yippie, zap (n.)

1969

acid freak, acquiree, ageism, aggro, Amerika, anarcho-capitalism, arcology, arte povera, bibliometrics, blahs, bot (= robot), breadhead, bunny-hop (v.), Chicana, Chicano, computeracy, cosmovision, cross-contaminate (v.), dashiki, debugger, dink, dolphinarium, econobox, exoticize, fine-tune (v.), gaslight (v.), grunt (U.S. soldier or marine), gunge, hands-on (adj.), hang time, hard-wired, homophobia, hood (= neighborhood), Imax, immunodeficiency, immunosuppress (v.), jockette, kitenge, liberation theology, Mailgram, medevac (v.), megastar, Mensan, Metroliner, mesc (= mescaline), microchip, microprocessor, middleware, midi, mimeo (v.), moonwalk (v.), mung (v.), Naderism, namaste (v.), (on the) natch, neocolonialization, networkable, Nixonomics, noodgy, nunchaku, off-roader, oncogene, oversell (n.), parasail (v.), Parsons table, pixel, plate tectonics, QED (quantum electrodynamics), quoadraphonic, quadraphony, ro-ro (= roll-on, roll-off, adj.), sado-maso (adj.), sexploit (v.), SFX (= sound effects), Sigint (= Signals intelligence), space shuttle, studly, techie, teeny, Vietnamization, Vietnamize, Waspdom, weaponization, windsurf (v.), Yalie, yech (interj.), zapper, zilch (v.)

Chapter 8

The Me Decade:

1970–1979

In an overview of the 1970s in *New York* magazine (August 23, 1976), the novelist Tom Wolfe described the '70s as the "*Me Decade*." It seems that people, weary of the chaotic conditions of the previous decade (but also influenced by the hippie counterculture of the '60s), turned away from social activism to activities that gave them solace or pleasure. Some became part of the *human potentials movement* by joining *encounter groups* like *est (Erhard Seminars Training)* and *Primal (Scream) Therapy;* others became members of religious cult groups like *Hare Krishna* and the *Jesus People;* still others pursued the cult of physical fitness by practicing *aerobics* or *Jazzercise.* The vast majority found escape in television, moviegoing, disco dancing, sports, and the like. This new, almost single-minded focus on self-fulfillment and self-gratification earned the generation of the 1970s the epithet the *Me Generation.*

"The premise of the 'me decade,'" summed up *Time* magazine (December 25, 1978), "is that great numbers of people are disdaining society to pursue existence as narcissistic massage buffs, *om*-sayers, encounter groupies." "Middle-class blacks have been seized by the 'Me Generation,'" reported the *New York Times Magazine* (December 3, 1978). "They are looking at themselves, their bodies, their minds, their golf swings, wardrobes and investment portfolios."

There was a notable exception to the inward-turning trend. In 1970, on the fiftieth anniversary of the Nineteenth Amendment, which gave women the right to vote, the *Women's Liberation movement* took wing and established itself as the most active organized social effort of the decade. *Women's Lib*, or *FemLib*, as the movement was informally known, called for the elimination of discriminatory practices against women in business, politics, and the arts. *Women's Liberationists* also introduced wide-ranging changes in the language, such as the removal of references to gender in texts (*degender* or *desex* the language), which focused especially on the suffix *-man* in words like *congressman, fireman, mailman, policeman, statesman*, presumably because they favored the male sex (even though historically *man* had the twofold meaning of "person" and "adult male"). As a result, during the 1970s, *Women's Libbers* succeeded in popularizing many nongender terms, such as *congressperson, firefighter, mail carrier, police officer, statesperson*.

The most popular substitution for both *-man* and *-woman* was the new combining form *-person*, used in dozens of compounds like *anchorperson, businessperson, chairperson, layperson, spokesperson, workperson*. The initial combining form *person-* was also used to substitute terms like *mankind, man-year, woman-year, man-day* with *personkind, person-year, person-day*. More popular were neutral substitutions, such as *flight attendant, housemaker, human-origin*, and *person Friday* for, respectively,

steward/stewardess, housewife, man-made, and *girl Friday*.
In addition, references to women considered sexist, such as
"the fair sex," "the better half," "the ball and chain," were
proscribed in style guides, while some militant feminists
went so far as to coin new terms to replace "sexist" conventional ones. A well-known coinage was *herstory* ("history
from the woman's viewpoint"), first used by the radical
feminist Robin Morgan in her 1970 book *Sisterhood Is
Powerful*; the coinage is a play on the word *history*, reinter-
preted as "his story." Another radical feminist coinage was
womyn, an alteration of *women* or *woman* to avoid the sexism perceived in the ending *-men* or *-man*.

Perhaps the most daring innovation in English by
the feminist movement was the attempt to institutional-
ize the common-gender (or genderless) pronoun *he/she* in
place of the generic *he* or the awkward substitute *he or
she*. A variant of *he/she* was *s/he*, as in *A patient can contact the doctor any time s/he wishes*. A common-gender
possessive form, *his/her*, was also introduced, as in *If
he/she is responsible, it's his/her duty to report the loss*. (To
avoid the entire issue of a genderless pronoun, some
writers have recommended the use of the "singular" *they*
and *their* in place of *he* and *his*, as in *If a student has a
complaint, they should take their problem to the teacher*;
but others consider this use ungrammatical and urge
writers to replace the singular phrase *If a student has*
with the plural *If students have*.)

The influence of Women's Lib was far-reaching in
the 1970s. It encouraged the formation of other libera-
tionist movements, such as *Gay Liberation* or *Gay Lib*,

which promoted gay civil rights and fought discrimination of gays and lesbians in business, politics, and the professions. It motivated animal lovers to fight for *animal liberation* or *animal lib*, which promoted *animal rights*, or the fair treatment of animals on moral grounds, and sought to protect animals from abuse or exploitation. In 1975, the American psychologist Richard D. Ryder coined the term *speciesism* (on the model of *sexism*) for the mistreatment and exploitation of certain animal species by humans. The adjective and noun *speciesist* was patterned after *sexist.* "Sexists and racists have been superseded by speciesists" (*New Scientist,* May 10, 1979).

Another exception to the inward-turning movements was the emergence of *environmentalism,* which was concerned with the effects of uncontrolled pollution of the earth's atmosphere. Some *environmentalists* (also called *antipollutionists* and *ecoactivists*) went beyond ecological concerns and rejected many technological advances, calling for "a return to a simple, pastoral life free of fumes, artificial chemicals and any noise but the chirping of birds" (*Science News,* June 19, 1971). To dramatize the need for pollution control, environmentalists established on April 22, 1970, *Earth Day,* during which activists throughout the world celebrated nature and demonstrated against its devastation through the wanton use of pollutants. In many large cities, Earth Day was extended to an entire week, named *Earth Week* and usually lasting from April 16 to April 22.

Also in 1970, the technical term *ecology,* referring to the balanced relationship between organisms and their

environment, took on a new political meaning of environmental concerns with the earth's atmosphere. Conse-
quently the prefix *eco-* came to mean "environmental" in
numerous new coined words, such as *ecoactivity, ecocatas-
trophe, ecocrisis, ecocide, ecodoom, ecopolitics.* A few disparaging terms using the prefix also found their way into
print, among them *ecofreak, econut,* and *ecopornographer*
(a publicist who exploits environmental concerns). But
ecocentrism, the focusing on environmental concerns over
other social issues, dominated much of the decade. For
example, the color *green* became associated with environmentalism in political organizations and movements like
the *Green Panthers, Greenpeace,* and the *Green Parties.*
Green was a translation of German *Grün,* used by the
Grünen (the "*Greens*"), a political party in West Germany devoted at first to campaigning against the building
of nuclear power plants, but then expanding into ecological and other political concerns.

The bad news in the 1970s was the widespread economic downturn that began with *stagflation,* a stagnant
condition of rising unemployment and spiraling inflation. Two other types followed during the decade: *hesifla-
tion,* a condition of spasmodic economic growth combined
with high inflation, and *slumpflation,* in which steady
inflation created and coexisted with a decline in business.
The latter condition was also dubbed *inflump,* a blend of
inflation and *slump.* In the mid-1970s an *energy crisis*
broke out, caused by a worldwide shortage in the supply
of oil and natural gas, causing *gas guzzlers* to run on
empty. An *odd-even* system of fuel rationing evolved, by

which car owners with odd-numbered license plates were sold gasoline only on odd-numbered days, alternating with car owners having even-numbered license plates.

The good news was the electronic revolution that brought on the development in the 1970s of the first *microprocessor* and *microcomputer*, the first *pocket calculator* (also called *minicalculator*), the first *video games* and *VCRs* (*videocassette recorders*), and the first *personal computers*. It also gave us the *hard disk* and *floppy disk* (or *diskette*) for storing data. But perhaps the greatest innovation of the decade was the creation of the *Internet*, the worldwide network of computers that facilitated the transmission of information across the globe.

In politics, the '70s suffered the biggest scandal in American history: *Watergate*. Before 1972, the name *Watergate* referred to an apartment, office, and hotel complex in Washington, D.C., built in 1967. In 1972, during the administration of President Richard M. Nixon, a group of men associated with efforts to reelect Nixon broke into the headquarters of the Democratic National Committee, which was located in the Watergate complex, in an attempt to burglarize it. Discovery of this crime brought to light a host of other crimes and misdemeanors that eventually led to President Nixon's resignation in 1974. The Watergate scandal not only made the name *Watergate* a generic term for political scandals, but spawned the combining form *-gate*, added to nouns and used throughout the '70s to mean any scandal involving abuse of power and its cover-up, such as *Irangate, Koreagate, Nannygate, Oilgate*—all nonce words used chiefly by newspapers and magazines to spice up their coverage of current news. The use of *-gate* survived into the 1980s: "The recent White House scandal [the Iran-Contra affair] has been a windfall for wordsmiths. . . . First came the five *-gates*: Reagan's Watergate, Reagangate, Irangate, Contragate, and Armsgate" (*American Speech*, Summer 1987).

Other combining forms of the decade fared better, leaving their mark on the evolving language. One of the long-lasting new combining forms of the '70s was *Euro-*, meaning "of or pertaining to Europe, the European Common Market, or the European money market," found in terms like *Eurocracy, Eurocrat, Eurocredit, Eurocurrency, Euronet, Europarliamentary*, which helped pave the way for the creation of the European monetary unit, the *euro*, in 1992.

Another enduring combining form of the '70s was *-aholic*, meaning "addicted to, excessively fond of or devoted to," as in *foodaholic, bookaholic, golfaholic, shopaholic, sexaholic, sweetaholic*. Variant forms are *-holic* and *-oholic*, as in *carboholic, chocoholic, cokeoholic, colaholic*. The combining form was derived from *workaholic*, coined by the American psychologist and educator Wayne Oates in 1971 from *work* + *-a-* + (alco)*holic*.

Still another combining form that became productive during the decade was *-athon*, derived from *marathon* and meaning "any prolonged activity or event requiring endurance," as in *bikeathon, spaceathon, workathon*. The variant *-thon* is used after a vowel, as in *discothon* (a contest among discotheque disk jockeys). The form and its variant were influenced by the much earlier *walkathon* (1932) and *telethon* (1949).

Americans discovered in the 1970s an American English dialect they hadn't known existed. It was *Black English* (1968), spoken by African Americans. The dialect, which linguists called *African American Vernaular English (AAVE)*, differed from standard American English in pronunciation, vocabulary, and grammar. Some examples of AAVE usage: *I be thinking. He be smart. We is friends. He my brover. I don't know nothin. I done it. He sleeping. Dey axed me to go. Hood* = neighborhood; *to diss* = to insult; *bad, baddest* = good, best. In 1973, linguists introduced the term *Ebonics* (a blend of *Ebony* and *phonics*) as a broader term than AAVE to encompass the various social dialects of black people in all English-speaking areas.

Also in the early 1970s, the ethnic name *African American* for a black American of African descent replaced such earlier names as *Afro-American, Negro*, and *Colored*. As a label of racial identity, *Black* attained prestige in the 1960s by its use in terms like *Black power, Black nationalism, Black English*, and the slogan *Black is beautiful*. A Black English idiom that came into general slang in the 1970s was *playing the dozens*, meaning a contest in which participants exchange insults about each other's relatives, especially their mothers. The contest is closely related to a verbal game called *signifying* or *sounding*, in which participants hurl teasing and usually insulting remarks against each other, the object being to top any preceding remark.

Popular culture in the '70s was dominated by television, whose fleeting and ephemeral shows contributed many passing whims, fads, and fashions. The term *couch potato* was invented in the mid-1970s for one whose main pastime is TV-watching. The term was intended as a pun on *boob tuber* (one who watches the *boob tube,* a 1960s slang term for television), *potato* being synonymous with *tuber.* One of the most popular shows of the decade was *All in the Family,* featuring the character *Archie Bunker,* an archtypical semiliterate working-class bigot whose extremism made him laughable and even endearing to millions. Among the favorite fads of the period were wearing *mood rings,* whose stone changed colors presumably with changes in the wearer's mood, and playing with *pet rocks,* small rocks treated like pets (a forerunner of the electronic "virtual pets" of the 1990s). One of the most widely publicized fads of the '70s was *streaking,* a stunt in which someone, usually a college student, dashes in the nude through a sports arena or other public place for no other purpose than to shock the bystanders or spectators; the verb *to streak* and the noun *streaker* derived from the stunt's name.

New amenities of the decade included the *hot tub,* an electrically heated tub of water, used for bathing or relaxation; the *karaoke* (from Japanese, literally, "empty orchestra"), entertainment in which a person sings along to recorded music, especially where the original vocals have been eliminated from the record; and the *hustle,* a dance for couples done to disco music, involving complicated footwork and spins. Other popular dances of the time were the *boogie,* a rock music version of the 1940s boogie-woogie, and the *salsa*, a Caribbean dance similar to the mambo but influenced by jazz and rock music. Various offshoots of rock music included *punk rock*, a loud, rowdy style in which performers wear garish makeup and bizarre clothes, a more restrained style called *new wave*, and the *heavy-metal* type of rock, with a heavy beat and amplified instrumental effects.

New fashions in women's clothing included the *Big Look*, which was loose and voluminous, the *layered look*, in which different garments are worn one over the other, strapless *bustiers*, and close-fitting *hot pants*.

In the art world, *conceptual art*, intended to reflect an idea or concept in the artist's mind in the process of creation, vied with other art forms, such as *arte povera* (from Italian, literally, "impoverished art"), in which the work is exhibited indirectly through photographs, descriptions, and so on; *fiber art*, consisting of three-dimensional structures shaped by weaving fibers on frames; and *fabric sculpture*, built up with pieces of fabric.

Religious revival movements emerged during the 1970s, chiefly among Protestants but also notably among followers of mystical Hindu and Sufi cults. The Protestant evangelical movement was often led by charismatic *televangelists*, and included *neo-Pentecostal* groups practicing spontaneous worship, the *Jesus People* (disparaged as *Jesus Freaks*), who were former hippies reborn as fervent evangelistic Christians, and *Jewish Christians*, such as the *Jews for Jesus* missionary group. The most conspicuous non-Christian group was the *Hare Krishna*, followers of the *Krishna Consciousness* movement devoted to the worship

of the Hindu god Krishna. Many standard new usages
came into the language during the decade, usually by processes such as abbreviation, back-formation, blending, borrowing, compounding, and derivation. Here is a list of the
processes, with a sampling of the new forms under them.

Abbreviations

*AI (artificial intelligence); aka (also known as); byob (bring
your own booze); CCU (coronary care unit); CPR
(cardiopulmonary resuscitation); DH (designated hitter);
DOE (Department of Energy); EPA (Environmental
Protection Agency); ER (emergency room); ERA (Equal
Rights Amendment); HMO (Health Maintenance
Organization); ICU (intensive care unit); IRA (Individual
Retirement Account); ISBN (International Standard Book
Number); MCP (male chauvinist pig); RV (recreational
vehicle); UPC (Universal Product Code); VCR (videocassette
recorder)*

*Acronyms (words formed from the first letters or
syllables of other words)*

*Ameslan (American Sign Language); AWACS (Airborne
Warning and Control System); COLA (cost of living
adjustment); MAD (Mutual Assured Destruction); MARV
(Maneuverable Reentry Vehicle); MEOW (moral equivalent of
war); OSHA (Occupational Safety and Health Administration);*

PINS (Person in Need of Supervision); RAM (random-access memory); SALT (Strategic Arms Limitation Talks); Taser (Tele-Active Shock Electronic Repulsion); TAPS (Trans-Alaska Pipeline System); WIN (Whip Inflation Now)

People often forget what the letters or syllables of an acronym stand for. The word *anacronym* (from *an-* "not, without" + *acronym*) was coined in the mid-1970s to designate acronyms that have become so common or familiar that almost no one knows what the letters originally stood for. For example, acronyms like *radar* (*radio detecting and ranging*), *laser, Taser, Swat, Opec, Wasp* are more accurately *anacronyms.*

Back-Formations

disgrunt, v.t. [1972, back-formed from *disgruntled*]; *house-sit* [1977, back-formed from *house-sitter*]; *safekeep, v.t.* [1972, back-formed from *safekeeping*]; *tumesce, v.* [1972, back-formed from *tumescence*]; *vasoligate, v.t.* [1973, back-formed from *vasoligation* (surgery to produce sterility)]

Blends

beautility (combined beauty and utility) [1973, blend of *beauty* and *utility*]; *beefalo* (a cross of cow and buffalo) [1974, blend of *beef* and *buffalo*]; *blaxploitation* (a film genre targeted to urban black audiences and starring primarily black actors) [1972, blend of *blacks* and *exploitation*]; *docutainment* (entertainment using documentary films) [1978, blend of *documentary* and *entertainment*]; *inflump* [1975, blend of *inflation* and *slump*]; *Motown* (style of rhythm and blues originating in Detroit) [1970, blend of *Motor* and *Town*]; *scrapnel* [1972, blend of *scrap* and *shrapnel*]; *yakow* (a cross of yak and cow) [1975, blend of *yak* and *cow*]; *zedonk* (a cross of zebra and donkey) [1971, blend of *zebra* and *donkey*]

Borrowings

bazaari (Iranian merchant) [1978, from Persian]; *calzone* (cheese-filled turnover) [1976, from Italian *calzoni* "trousers"]; *Chicana* (Mexican American female) [1972, from Mexican Spanish, feminine of Chicano]; *gulag* (forced labor camp in the Soviet Union) [1974, from Russian]; *hapkido* (Korean martial art) [1971, from Korean, literally, "way of harmonious force"]; *kwanza* (African American cultural festival) [1971, from Swahili]; *salsa* (Caribbean dance music) [1975, from American Spanish, literally, "sauce"]; *samizdat* (underground press) [1977, from Russian, literally, "self-publishing"]

Clippings (words formed by shortening other words, as by clipping syllables)

mesc [1970, short for *mescaline*]; *muni* (municipal bond) [1973, short for *municipal*]; *quad* [1974, short for

quadrillion]; *romcom* (romantic comedy, patterned on
sitcom) [1971, short for *romantic comedy*]; *teenie* [1971,
short for *teenager*]; *trank* [1972, short for *tranquilizer*]

Coined words (words created or invented for a particular purpose)

Catch-22 (a perplexing dilemma or paradox) [1971, coined by
U.S. writer Joseph Heller]; *cellulite* (fatty substance forming
lumps on the surface of thighs, buttocks, etc.) [1971, coined
by French dietitian Nicole Ronsard, from French *cellule*
"cell"]; *decidophobia* (avoidance of decision making) [1972,
coined by the U.S. philosopher Walter Kaufmann]; *factoid*
(something unsubstantiated taken as fact) [1973, coined by
U.S. writer Norman Mailer]; *gazillion* (a very large number
greater than a zillion) [1978]; *granola* (breakfast cereal or
snack) [1970, coined as a trademark, probably from Italian
grano "grain" + suffix *-ola*]; *humongous* (extremely big,
tremendous) [1970, slang coinage, apparently a blend of
huge and *monstrous*]; *psychobabble* (psychoanalytic jargon)
[1977, coined by U.S. author Richard D. Rosen]; *speciesism*
(discrimination against various animal species) [1975, coined
by U.S. psychologist Richard D. Ryder]

Compounds

bag lady (homeless old woman) [1977]; *ballpark figure*
(rough estimate) [1972]; *Big Look* (women's clothing

fashion) [1974]; *docudrama* (documentary-style dramatization) [1976]; *downsize* (reduce in size) [1975]; *Greenpeace* (environmentalist movement) [1977]; *off-the-wall* (unconventional) [1974]; *personkind* (human race, mankind) [1972]; *rip-off* (theft, swindle, racket) [1970]; *skatepark* (area set aside for skateboarding) [1976]

Shifts (changes in parts of speech or meanings)

access (to obtain access to) [1970, verb from noun]; *clone* (carbon copy, replica) [1978, figurative meaning of *clone* "plant duplicated asexually"]; *excess* (to dismiss an employee due to overstaffing) [1976, verb from noun]; *geriatric* (a geriatric patient) [1974, noun from adjective]; *lesion* (to cause a lesion) [1972, verb from noun]

Expressions

do a number on (play a trick or joke on) [1974]; *get one's act together* (get organized) [1978]; *give a for instance* (give an example) [1971]; *on the back burner* (of secondary or subordinate importance) [1973]; *on the front burner* (of primary or immediate importance) [1970]; *on the money* (on the nose, on target) [1971]; *run with the ball* (to advance a plan, venture, etc.) [1971]; *take a bath* (suffer a loss) [1970]; *twist in the wind* (be very uncertain, endure great suspense) [1974]

A Selection of New Words of the 1970–1979 Decade

1970

adhocracy, adversarial, ageist, air-con, Amex, arte povera, auto-destruction, Big Mac, biofeedback, Chicanismo, citizen advocacy, counterculture, dehire (v.), detox (v.), disintermediate (v.), dorky, eco-political, eco-politics, factionalize, 'fro (= Afro), funkadelic, hahnium, halloumi cheese, Hare Krishna (movement), herstory, hot pants, humongous, kalashnikov, Jesus Freak, Kirlian (photography), labradoodle, Lassa fever, Lib, longuette, Lunokhod, Marsokhod, mau-mau (v.), medicalization, mediocritization, metaphorization, microsociety, migrationism, mi'jita, mind-expander, minidisk, monstro, mold-breaking, Muppet, Naderite, Nerf, newbie, no-lose (adj.), notaphilist, notaphily, off-put (v.), off-roading, ohmigod, Orwellism, pervo (adj.), polyversity, poopy, power trip, preprogram, primal scream, punk rock, quadraphonic, quadrasonic, relaunch (n.), repo man, rip-off (n., adj.), Sallie Mae (SLMA), schmatte, scientificity, shambolic, shockumentary, sickout, Skylab, sound-alike, telemedicine, turista, uptick, vibraharp, wallbanger, yucky

1971

Amtrak, animatronics, Asperger's syndrome, bioethics, biogas, bong, boy toy, bubble wrap, chairperson, clip art, codependence, djembe, ecotage, Euro, fabby, fabric sculpture, fajita, freeline (v.), gluon, gonzo, gyro, hapkido, heightism, heightist, homesitter, house-sit (v.), immunodeficient, Jones (v.), Jesus People, KREEP (lunar elements), Kwanza/ Kwanzaa (African American festival), libber, Maffei (galaxy), magcon, microwaved, Mirandize, motherboard, moto, narratee, narratology, nutball, oillionaire, peer review, phone phreak, phreak (n., v.), pimpmobile, polydrug (adj.), postminimal, postminimalism, pro-life (adj.), quadrominium, romcom, sambuca, sizeism, sizeist, superfly (adj.), tataki, televangelist, ultrafiche, video (v.), Wiccan (adj., n.), yikes (interj.), zedonk

1972

Ameslan, amped (adj.), Archie Bunker, Atkins (diet), biathlete, binge eat (v.), blaxploitation, capo di tutti capi, chile poblano, chocoholic, congressperson, de-accession (v.), driveability, ecocentric, ecoteur, Eurocentrist, feel-good (adj., n.), fiber art, flexitime/flextime, floppy disk, gasohol, gentrify, gorp, Greenpeace, guilt trip, gut-wrenching (adj.), hardscape, high-tech, Inupiaq, JAP (Jewish American Princess), Jewish Christian, Jews for Jesus, Latina, layered look, layperson, lumpectomy, mail bomb, mediocritize, miniseries, moodscape, motorcross, muggee, personkind, pro-lifer, punk rocker, RICO (Racketeer Influenced and

Corrupt Organizations), salsero, Singlish, smiley face,
spokesperson, superfecta, Taser, transdenominational,
Vegeburger, viewshed, winability/winnability, Zairean, zonky

1973

ambisonic, aspartame, benchmarking (n.), breatharianism,
Cal-Mex (adj.), carbo (n.), cinephilia, deconstruct (v.),
diskette, Ebonics, ecotour, est (Erhard Seminars Training),
factoid (n., adj.), foreperson, 4WD (four-wheel drive),
F-word, gas guzzler, gentrification, heavy-metal, hot tub,
jubbly, mainstream (v.), mediagenic, motorhead, muni
(= municipal), newsfeed, nutso, open date, perinatology,
petrodollar, plea-bargain (v.), sexploitative, spiroplasma, Sri
Lankan, streaking, surimi, Symbionese, televangelist, temp
(v.), tonto, triathlon, Ultrasuede, Unix, weird out, what-if,
workshop (v.), wushu, Yerkish, zipless

1974

acupoint, affordably, bankerly, bar-hopper, beefalo, Bikram
yoga, carpaccio, closed captioning, computerphobe,
cryopreserve (v.), desertification, destabilization, Dungeons &
Dragons, ethnocide, floss (v.), genethics, genogram,
heli-skiing, home-sitting, hosebag, Internet, Kevlar,
leptoquark, mainstream (v.), marzipan (v.), materials scientist,
meds (= medications), metafictional, metafictionist,

meterage, migawd, Minihole, mini-mall, mixmaster (v.),
monoculturation, moonie, nanotechnology, narratologist,
neomort, Nuyorican, Nicorette, Nikkei (index), Nova (lox),
number-crunch (v.), packetization, packetize, parallel park
(v.), parm (= parmigiana), peopleware, popmobility,
posedown, quad (= quadriplegic), retro (n., adj.), rotavirus,
scrungy, seitan, Sensurround, sick-in, slumpflation,
spokespeople, sportsplex, transgender (adj., n.), trifecta,
ultralight, vox (= vocals), Zairese

1975

abductee, affluential, air-kiss (v.), anacronym, auteurist,
bashert, bean-counter, brown dwarf, CAT (computer-assisted
tomography), closed caption, conspiracist, craftspeople,
cruciverbalist, customization, deconflict (v.), deregulatory,
detox (n.), downsize (v.), ecotopia, ecotopian, fractal (adj., n.),
fundie, glassification, glassify, hustle (dance), keypad,
mastectomee, McDonaldization, mediacracy, medicalize,
medigap, micromanagement, minceur (n., adj.), mini
(= mini-computer), minimalize, mood ring, moonball,
motherese, motocrosser, multiculturism, narratological,
needlepoint (v.), nut job, ombudsperson, onomasticism,
outcall, peer review (v.), pet rock, phallocentrism, phallocrat,
phallocratic, playlist, Post-it, post-structuralism,
psychobabble, refusenik, rope-a-dope, salsa, sinsemilla,

speciesism, telecomputer, transition (v.), trash-talking (adj.), underperform, Vaticanology, veggie, viewdata, Vuitton, wetware, womyn

---

1976

back-burner (v.), backlisted, barbie (= barbecue), Bollywood, boomer (= baby boomer), brainiac, bulimarexia, buyout, classist (adj., n.), commoditized, datagram, demotivate, droid (= android), Ebola virus, ecocentrism, ecomuseum, endorphin, espresso macchiato, Ethernet, fembot, fly-through, garbology, gigaflop, gloppy, hard disk, hospice, Inuktitut, Islamophobia, Jazzercize, Kampuchean (= Cambodian), keyboardist, Legionnaires' disease, Lyme (disease), mailmobile, megaflop, meme, memic, mentor (v.), mesclun, microcassette, mindstyle, mini-bar, minichain, munchkin, narcology, neo-Pentecostalist, networker, no-tell motel, nouvelle cuisine, nowcasting, old moneyed (adj.), orature, out-year, PIN (personal identification number), playtime, potty-train (v.), public key, punkster, rejectionist, retrovirus, roach motel, Shake'n'Bake, signage, skeevy (adj.), sleazoid (adj., n.), soulster, statesperson, telenovela, vermiculture, vested (adj.), wuss, yahoo (interj.), zeppole

---

1977

agribiz, agriproduct, animatic, autobiopic, biocomputing, boogie board (type of surfboard), born-again (= reborn, reconverted), 'burb (= suburb), catfight (v.), channel-hop (v.), chemo (= chemotherapy), cocksmanship, desaparecido, download (n.), drama-doc (= drama-documentary), Eisbock, Euronote, fast-track (v.), guilt-trip (v.), gravitino, heptathlon, high-maintenance (adj.), incent (v.), incentivization, incrementalist, jet-skiing, kwanza (monetary unit), limerence, limerent, log-on (n.), loose cannon, lowball (v.), MEGO (my eyes glaze over), mikeside (n.), minicamp, mono (= monohull), montology, move-up buyer, munchy, nanocomputer, nekkid, neotenize, 900 number, nip and tuck (n.), no-name (adj.), new wave (music), nowcast (n.), nubile (n.), outperformance, pain de mie, palimony, parcours(e), phallocracy, phone phreaker, punker, rockumentary, s/he, soca, Steadicam, sicko, wacko (adj., n.), wedgie, white-bread (adj.), wussy

1978

anthemic, anti-choice, bar-hopping (adj.), bioinformatics, closed captioned, computeresque, coupledom, courseware, ditsy, docutainment, ecotoxic, FOAF (Friend of a Friend), gazillion, giveback (n.), hacky-sack (n.), internet (v.), job-share (v.), lookism, lookist, luggable, machete (v.), magalogue, malling, maquiladora, maxed, me-ism, mentoring, Mexamerica, midweeker, mini (n.), monkeywrencher, mule (v.), neo-Pentecostalism, noogie, op (= opportunity), overhype, overtop (prep.), paragliding,

parasail, pigout, pod person, POSSLQ (person of opposite
sex sharing living quarters), psychobilly, psychonaut,
punkabilly, punked, reboot (v.), roller-ski, sell-through,
slomo (= slow motion), snitty, telco (= telecommunication),
text message, upsize (v.), videophile, voicebank, wonky

1979

amp (v.), ahistorical, arrabbiata (sauce), at sign (= @),
backlist (v.), booze cruise, breathrian (n.), bustier (n.),
channel hopper, channel hopping, claymation, close-
caption/closed-caption (v.), codependent, commodize,
cowpunk, C-word, deal breaker, deejaying, detangle (v.),
eurozone, First Worlder, free-base (v.), French-braid (v.),
ground truthing, hardscaping, high concept, improv
(= improvisation), insourcing, intranet, karaoke, machoism,
McDonaldize, mediacrat, medspeak, megamoney,
mellowspeak, motormouthed, nebbishy, ne-con (adj.), New
Ager, nukespeak, omakase (menu choice made by chef),
overhype (v.), p2p (= person to person), partied-out, pepper
spray, perimortem (adj.), pester power, playlist (v.), pod
people, prosumer (= consumer-producer), road-kill (v.),
trendoid (adj.), Twinkie defense, umami (flavor), upload
(n.), Walkman, z-list (least important list)

Chapter 9

The Yuppie Generation:

1980–1989

Tom Wolfe, who coined the phrase the Me Decade for the 1970s, named the baby boomers of the 1980s "the splurge generation," referring to the purchasing habits of the new career-minded twenty-to-thirty-year-old professionals who earned large salaries and lived in a conspicuously affluent manner. Wolfe's new phrase didn't catch on; instead, by the mid-1980s, the group that came of age in the Me Decade got to be called the *Yuppie generation,* as in this 1985 film review: "Movies for and about the Yuppie generation . . . have tended to be equally self-interested and out of touch with the rest of the world—being fatuous, self-important and humorless examinations of the mini-problems of the young, restless well-to-do" (Vincent Canby, *New York Times,* August 14, 1985).

It was in 1984 that *Yuppie* became the pet name and standard sobriquet of a member of the young urban professionals who took over Wall Street, Madison Avenue, Fifth Avenue, and their equivalents outside New York. The name was popularized by *The Yuppie Handbook: The State-of-the-Art Manual for Young Urban Professionals,* by Marissa Piesman and Marilee Hartley, which filled bookstores in 1984 as a clone of the best-selling *Official Preppy Hand-*

book (1980), an entertaining paperback about the spoiled-rich lifestyle of preppies popularized by the 1970 film *Love Story*. The word *Yuppie* (often spelled *yuppie*) was formed from the initial letters of *Young urban professional* (or a popular variant, *Young upwardly mobile professional*) + the suffix *-ie*, on the model of the 1960s *hippie* and *yippie* (a politically active hippie, from *YIP*, abbreviation of *Youth International Party*, a name of the yippie group).

"Who are those upwardly mobile folks with designer water, running shoes, pickled parquet floors and $450,000 condos in semislum buildings?" asked rhetorically *Time* magazine of January 9, 1984. Its answer: "Yuppies, of course, for Young Urban Professionals. . . . Yuppies are dedicated to the twin goals of making piles of money and achieving perfection through physical fitness and therapy." The name spawned various subspecies, such as *buppies* (black Yuppies) and *guppies* (gay Yuppies), as well as derivatives like *Yuppiedom, Yuppieism, yuppification*, and *yuppify*.

Yuppie women were dubbed *yuppettes*. A running joke had a yuppette marry a yuppie stockbroker. When asked how they met, she replied, "We were introduced by a mutual fund." Woman yuppies became *power dressers,* sporting masculine-cut outfits suggesting competence, self-confidence, and power. To enhance their appearance, female (and often male) yuppies resorted to new cosmetic treatments, such as *self-tanning lotions, tanning booths, liposuction*, and injections of wrinkle-smoothing *Botox*. But women's role in the '80s spanned across the workplace into such areas as politics and environmentalism. A successful political action organization, *Emily's List,* was formed in 1983 to help elect women running for public office, the name *Emily* being an acronym of *Early Money Is Like Yeast* (from a political fund-raising saying, "Early money is like yeast; it helps to raise the dough"). *Ecofeminism,* a movement linking environmental issues with feminism, gained prominence in 1980. *Ecofeminists* claimed that there was a strong connection between the male subordination of women in many societies and their depredation and exploitation of nature.

The rise of the Yuppie generation coincided with the two-term presidency of Ronald Reagan (1981–1989), known both for his economic policies (*Reaganomics*) and a presidential tenure unscathed by scandal (*Teflon presidency,* named after the "nonstick" chemical coat on cookware). The mid-decade saw the end of the Cold War and the dissolution of the Soviet Union through the new policies of *glasnost* (openness) and *perestroika* (restructuring), which in turn led to the collapse of Communist governments in East Germany, Czechoslovakia, Hungary, Poland, and Romania. These factors combined to end the previous decade's economic "slumpflation"and usher in an era of binge spending signaled by the *ka-ching* of cash registers ringing up sales.

The boom benefited the budding electronic and computer industries, which produced in 1980 the *compact disk* (*CD*), in 1983 the *Windows* operating system for personal computers, and in 1981 the electronic communications network *BITNET* linking most universities in the United States and Canada. In 1982, the short form *e-mail* for *electronic mail* was used for the first time, and the first *cellphone* was made available in 1984 for a suggested price of $1,995. The *palmtop* computer ("small enough to hold on the palm of the hand") was invented in 1987, the *e-book* (a book in electronic format) was predicted in 1988, and the information-retrieval systems *infobot* (from *info* + [ro]*bot*) and *knowbot* were introduced in 1986 and 1988, respectively. With the spread of computers came the *hackers,* skilled programmers who *infected* computer programs or networks with *viruses,* subprograms that replicate themselves and spread to other programs or computers: "Computer viruses . . . can destroy data, display an unexpected message, make a disk unusable, or wreak some other form of havoc" (*Philadelphia Inquirer,* March 27, 1988).

Computer viruses weren't the worst news of the '80s. The worst nuclear accident in history occurred on April 26, 1986, when the Chernobyl nuclear power plant exploded in the Soviet Union, releasing hundreds of times more fallout than the 1945 atomic bombing of Hiroshima. Just months before Chernobyl, on January 28, 1986, the U.S. space program had its greatest setback when the space shuttle *Challenger* disintegrated after launch, causing the death of all seven astronauts aboard. These disasters were matched only by the eruption of the most deadly disease of the decade, *AIDS* (*acquired immune deficiency syndrome*), whose existence was first reported in 1981 under various names before the U.S. Centers for Disease Control and Prevention (CDC) settled on the current name in September 1982. AIDS was an epidemic transmitted by a retrovirus, *HIV* (*human immunodeficiency virus*), which was first identified in 1986. Many talented people succumbed to AIDS in the 1980s, among them the fashion designer Perry Ellis, the actor Rock Hudson, the entertainer Liberace, and the photographer Robert Mapplethorpe. Science came to the rescue in the mid-1990s with the introduction of HAART (*highly active antiretroviral therapy*), which saved the lives of AIDS victims in the developed world, though in parts of Africa and Asia it is still fatal to millions.

Another scourge of the '80s was the steep rise of cocaine addiction with the increasing use in 1985 of a potent form of coke called *crack* or *rock*. This was cocaine that was *freebased*, that is, heated and concentrated in pellets for inhaling or smoking. Addicts of this pure and extremely addictive drug were known as *crackheads*, and a place where crack could be bought or sold was a *crack house*. The trade in illegal drugs reached new heights during the decade, often abetted by South American drug traffickers known as *narcotraficantes*. The combining form *narco-* (from *narcotics*) generated numerous new words throughout the decade to denote the business or trade of illegal drugs, among them *narcodollars, narcomillionaire, narcotrafficking, narcocrime, narcoterrorism,* and *narcoterrorist.*

On a brighter side of the decade, a popular youth culture evolved, which flaunted new musical tastes and habits, such as listening or watching the *MTV* cable television network hosted by *video jockeys* (*VJs*), walking or traveling with *Walkman* audio players stuck to their ears, dancing the Brazilian *lambada,* and introducing such novelties as *slam dancing,* in which dancers *moshed* or collided purposefully with each other. The young of the inner cities played *rap music* on *boom boxes* (also called *ghetto blasters*), and popularized *hip-hop,* a subculture incorporating diverse elements, such as *rapping, break-dancing, beat-boxing* (vocalizing instrumental sounds), and *graffiti art.* Other influences on the popular culture were electronic *video arcade* games like *Pac-Man* (who devours opponents); the *Nintendo* home video games, among them *Game Boy*; and mechanical puzzles like *Rubik's cube* (invented by Ernö Rubik, a Hungarian sculptor). The games' popularity was underscored in 1989 when the entire generation of young players was renamed the *Nintendo generation,* an epithet that has lived into the next century (the *OED* includes a 2003 citation for the phrase).

Here are some other new terms that emerged in the 1980s:

24-7, adv. [1985]. Numerical shorthand for "24 hours a day, 7 days of the week"; (open) at all times, (available) constantly: *The office is accessible 24-7.* "McDonald's went 24/7 in Garner in April, 2005, after a push by corporate headquarters to boost profits by extending store hours" (*BusinessWeek,* February 5, 2007). *Usage Note:* Now often used in commercial titles, such as *24-7 Wall Street, 24/7 Entertainment, 24-7 Real Estate.*

anime, n. [1985]. From Japanese, from French *animé* "animated." A Japanese animated cartoon, usually featuring science fiction or fantasy.

benji or Benji, n. [1985]. Pet name for *Benjamin*, after *Benjamin* Franklin, whose image is on a $100 bill. Slang. A $100 bill.

ecotourism, n. [1982]. Travel to natural areas that conserve the environment and preserve the well-being of local people: "Costa Rica is practically synonymous with the term 'ecotourism,' and for good reason. Misty cloud forests, black sand beaches and rushing river rapids offer outdoor activities for both casual nature enthusiasts and hardcore adventure travelers."(MSNBC, April 19, 2007).—ecotourist, n. [1985]

gridlock, n. [1980]. Total stoppage of all traffic when long lines of vehicles block major intersections; a major traffic jam: "*Gridlock* quickly replaced such tired terminology as logjam, bumper-to-bumper, glut of cars, wall-to-wall parking lot" (*New York Daily News*, April 13, 1980).

high-five, n. [1980]. A gesture of greeting or congratulation in which two people slap each other's palms and fingers with their arms raised above waist level. Compare *low-five*.

Hummer. [1983]. From *Hum(vee)* + *-er*. A brand of four-wheel-drive, off-road vehicles developed from the military *Humvee* [1982, acronym for *HMMWV* (High-Mobility Multipurpose Wheeled Vehicle)].

infotainment, n. [1980]. From *info*(rmation) + (enter)*tainment*. Any communication system, especially television or radio broadcasting, that combines information and entertainment.

low-five, n. [1982]. A gesture of greeting or congratulation in which two people slap each other's palms and fingers with their arms below waist level. Compare *high-five*.

McDonald's, n. [1982]. After the *McDonald's* fast-food chain. Any highly standardized and efficiently marketed operation or business, as in *the McDonald's of information services.*

McWord, n. [1982]. From *Mc*(Donald's) + *Word*. Any word coined to suggest a similarity to the cheap, quick standardized serving of fast food by the McDonald's chain, such as *McFashion, McPaper, McTheater, McNews.*

mediascape, n. [1987]. From *media* + -*scape* ("extensive view or perception"). The view or perception conveyed by the communications or mass media, as in *a survey of the American mediascape, a mediascape of the election campaign.*

monkeywrenching, n. [1985]. From the phrase *throw a monkey wrench into the works*; "to interfere with the smooth operation of machinery." Sabotage for environmental reasons, intended to stop or interfere with a business or industry regarded as destructive to the environment: "Monkeywrenching is a step beyond civil disobedience. It is nonviolent, aimed only at inanimate objects. It is one of the last steps in defense of the wild, a deliberate action taken by an Earth defender when almost all other measures have failed" (*Earth First! Journal*, December 2008).

moonwalk, n. [1983]. A dance move that suggests walking forward while actually walking backward, popularized by the pop-music star Michael Jackson (1958–2009).—*v.i.* To execute a moonwalk. "The amazing thing, in retrospect, is that he moonwalked only twice during the performance" (*Boston Globe*, July 2, 2009).

retronym, n. [1980]. From *retro-* "backward" + *(o)nym* "name." A new name created for an old word to clarify its meaning, usually by modifying the old word with an adjective, as *skim milk* or *nonfat milk* (for *milk*), *push-button phone* or *rotary phone* (for *phone*). ". . . that refreshing and pleasantly inexpensive drink, not carbonated but with its own beaded bubbles winking at the brim, is now known by the retronym *tap water*" (William Safire, *New York Times*, January 7, 2007).

threequel, n. [1983]. Blend of *three* and *sequel*, on the model of *prequel* (1973). The third of a series of works; a sequel to a sequel: "In 2007, theater marquees will be dominated by a particular numeral, thanks to a release schedule that includes **Spider-Man 3, Pirates of the Caribbean 3, Shrek 3, Bourne 3, Rush Hour 3**. This may be the year of the threequel, but not all the franchises will be successful" (*Christian Science Monitor,* January 5, 2007).

Valleyspeak or Valspeak, n. [1982]. The slang used by teenagers of the San Fernando Valley in Southern California, as in *omigod! grody to the max* ("extremely gross"), *awesome, fer shirr! Hey, like wow, this is for me! Usage Note: Valleyspeak* was popularized in the 1980s and influenced U.S. teenage speech into the 1990s and beyond.

wannabe, n., adj. [1981]. From the informal pronunciation of *want to be.* A person who aspires to emulate a celebrity in appearance, career, style, etc.: *a Madonna wannabe.* "Wannabe Space Tourist Wants $21 Million Back Over Scuttled Mission" (*Wired,* September 24, 2008).

A Selection of New Words of the 1980–1989 Decade

1980

air guitar, biochip, bird flu, boardsailing (= sailboarding), boot (v., a computer), carbo-loading, comb-over (n.), computer disk, dis (v., = disrespect), download (v.), ecofeminism, electronica (music), Euro (adj.), exfiltrate (v.), freebase (n., v.), the frizzies, gazillionaire, gridlock (n., adj.), hazmat (n.), high-five, infotainment, Islamophobic, jet skier, ka-ching (interj.), magret (meat fillet), Marielito, mathlete (= math athlete), mojado (= wetback), moqueca (fish stew), mountain bike, multiplex (cinema), narcotraficante, nerdish, Nimby (not in my back yard), originalism, pair-bond (v.), paraflight, plex (= multiplex), popism (pop art), power dresser, Reaganomics, robata (grill), roid (= steroid), Rubik's cube, self-tanning, slobbish, super-max (prison), tanning booth, teleport, usageaster, veg (= vegetate), waitperson, waitron

---

1981

ableism, aliteracy, b-boy or b-girl (= break dancer), BITNET, boom box, carb (= carbohydrate), chill pill, computerate (= computer-literate), cyberphobia, def (adj., = excellent), dockominium, dope (adj., = excellent), emergicenter, Euroland, geeky, groupware, home-school (adj.), home-schooler, hot-list (v.), infomercial, LAN (Local Area Network), MADD (Mothers Against Drunk

Driving), martial artist, merengue (v.), microcode (v.), motormouthing, MTV (music television), mud-wrestle (v.), multicast (adj., n.), narcoleptocracy, outsourcing, Pac-Man, perp, petit-mort, popist (= pop artist), portastudio, rap music, rapping, reboot (n.), Sendero Luminoso, SFX (= special effects), Stepford (adj.), trash talk, Walkman, wannabe (n., adj.), wimp (v.), wussy (adj., n.)

1982

aero (= aerodynamic), aerobicize, AIDS (aquired immune deficiency syndrome), backslash (\), barista, bimbette, bodyboard, camcorder, carbo-load (n., adj.), CD (computer disk), cellulitic, club-hop (v.), co-branded (credit card), cyberphobe, cyberspace, dangdut (music), dollarization, dweeb, ecotourism, e-mail, exoticization, foodie, gaydar, gridlock (v.), grody, heli-ski (adj., v.), hip-hop (n., adj.), Humvee, Islamophobe, low-five, McDonald's, megastore, microbrewery, microwavable, morph (v.), mouseburger, multicast (v.), multitasker, Netter, netiquette, party animal, pedometry, photoaging, pixelated, pixelation, pleather, power walking, redial (n.), sabermetrics, scrollable, skanky, skell (n.), soccer mom, spreadsheet, taqueria, teenspeak, text messaging, thrashy, tiramisu, triathlete, Valleyspeak, veejay or VJ (= video jockey), video arcade, word-process (v.), wysiwyg (what you see is what you get), xeriscape, yeek (interj.)

1983

adware, aerobicize (v.), air guitar (v.), avian flu, beatboxing, bodyboarder, -bot, break-dance (v.), build down, carbo-load (v.), computerphobic, cryptid, cyberpunk, D.A.R.E. (Drug Abuse Resistance Education), deejay (v.), defragment (v.), DNR (do not resuscitate), dumpster diving, edutainment, exfoliant (n., adj.), Five-O (police officer), flamage, future-proof (adj.), ghetto blaster, glitchy, greenmail, (computer) hacker, heli-skier, hot key, Hummer, jet-ski (v.), liposuction, meg (= megabyte), microbrewer, mojo (sauce), mosh (v.), moonwalk (n., v.), motormouth (v.), mud-wrestle (n.), multicast (n.), Nazi skin (= skinhead), nerdiness, nerdishness, newsgroup, niching, no-tech (adj.), obesogenic, pannist, perma-tanned, pie-hole, polystylist, pooch (v.), post-feminism, pre-AIDS, prenup, propeller-head, quadrathlon, slam dancing, spell-check (v., n.), surtitle, sysop (= system operator), Teflon (adj.), threequel, trannie (= transvestite), transgender (adj., n.), transgendered, transgenderism, urgicenter (= emergicenter), veganic, voice-over (v.)

1984

add-in (adj., n.), AIDS-related complex, big whoop (= big deal), bodyboarding, boink (v.), boogie boarder (= bodyboarder), boogie boarding, breakbeat, bubble-wrap (v.), buppie (= black Yuppie), cellphone, com

(= commercial Internet site), computer virus, detectorist
(= metal detectorist), disablist, DJ-ing, double-click (v.),
Eurosclerosis, fab (= fabrication), freakazoid (n., adj.),
geekiness, ground-truth (v.), guppie (= gay Yuppie), home-
school (v.), kill file, Mac (= Macintosh computer), MC-ing,
midhusband, mimeticism, minarchist, minarchy, modemed,
mousse (v.), nanocrystal, nanocrystalline, neckdown,
Nethead, netizen, outsourced, paintball, perma-tan,
phreaker, point woman, plore (n.= explore), plug-and-play,
pop tart (pop star), quinzhee (snow shelter), shopaholic,
Singlish, sneakernet, snowboarder, snowboarding, telnet (v.),
teraflop, WIMP (window, icon, mouse, program), wuss, Yap
(Young aspiring professional), yumpie (young upwardly
mobile person), Yuppie (young urban professional),
Yuppiedom, Yuppieism, yuppification, yuppify, Zelig

1985

abortuary, Aerobie, aerobrake, app (= application), benji
(= Benjamin, $100 bill), big box (warehouse), bigorexia,
bookmarking, boxercise, clickable, cosmeceutical, crash-
and-burn, dosha (Ayurvedic humors), double click (n.),
downwinder, dumpster-dive (v.), dumpster-diver, ecotourist,
Emily's list, garmento, geekdom, gendercide, glasnost,
go-to (adj.), hot-key (v.), intifada, japanimation (= anime),
Krav Maga (contact combat), mifky-pifky (= hanky-panky),

minilab, mosh (n.), narcocracy, Nettie, noirish, N-word,
offshore (v.), overamped, PostScript, power shopping,
power-walk (v.), power-walker, problemo, Prozac, Rambo,
Ramboesque, Rollerblade, skatepunk, snarfle (v.), statin,
tankini, 24-7 (n.)

1986

AIDS virus, backlisting, basehead (crack addict),
bookmarked, Botox, break dancing, channel-surf (v.), channel
zapper, defragmenter, dinky (double income no kids), dis (n.,
insult), DJ (v.), dolee, dress-down (adj.), e-mailable, e-mailer,
e-mailing, feel-bad (adj.), foot-shooting (n.), future-proof (v.),
guido, HIV (human immunodeficiency virus), hot-link (v.),
iconify, infobot, infoholic, internetwork (v.), ish (adv.), McJob,
mell of a hess, motormouthing (adj.), multitask (v.),
namecheck (v.), nanoscale, neoconceptualism, neo-noir (adj.,
n.), New Agey (adj.), nice (v.), outercourse, perestroika,
pixmap, po-mo (= postmodernism), power shopper, power
walk, scenester, sippy cup, skeeve (v.), tech-head, twelve-step
(v.), trash talker, v-mail (= voice mail), woopie (well-off older
person), zaitech, zouk (music)

1987

aerobot, bazillionaire, beatboxing, Bikram (yoga), Bork (v.),
defragger, defragmentation, dink (= dinky), dissing (n.),

e-mail (v.), fattism, geekfest, geekhood, genetic fingerprint, gengineer, gengineering, genomics, grafitti (v.), greenwash, hella (= helluva), info-dump, izakaya (bar, café), long-termism, long-termist, machohood, mass-customize, mediascape, metal detectorist, monobrow, munged, nanotech (adj., n.), neurocomputer, neurocomputing, New Ageism, Nintendo, nummies (= goodies), off-label (adj., adv.), offshoring, ollie (v.), outsourcer, palmtop (n., adj.), paraglide, parapente, photo-radar, Pixelvision, po-mo (= postmodern, postmodernist), power-dress (v.), propeller-headed, prosumer (= professional consumer), pubcaster (= public broadcaster), punditocracy, pyro (= pyrotechnics), ragazine, rightsize (v.), sandboarding, smiley (= smiley face), smiley face, tabloidesque, technopreneur, virtual reality, warez (n.)

1988

acid house (music), acid jazz, alt (= alternate), beatbox (v.), blunt (cigar), boo (= beau, sweetheart), Borking (n.), Cantopop (music), cell (= cell phone), channel graze (v.), channel-surfing, channel-surfer, c-branding, cohousing, cugine, defrag (n., v.), e-book, 800-number, faxback, F-bomb, fiend (v.), gangsta (n., adj.), genetic fingerprinting, hanger steak, himbo (= him bimbo), hip-house (music), hydrospeed, hyperlink (n., v.), infect (computers), karoshi, knowbot, Kuiper belt, lambada, liposculpture, marma, microchip, micromachine, modem (v.), mommy track, multi (= multiplex), New Beat, no-fly zone, noodging (adj.), ordie (= ordnance handler), paraglide, paralympian, parapenting, rageaholic, road rage, swingbeat, techno (n., adj.), threepeat (n.), twelve-stepper, (computer) vaccination, xeriscaper

1989

abdominizer, beat-down (n, = beating), boxaerobic, Britpopper, cosmo (= cosmopolitan), couply (adj.), crowd surfing, Cyberia (= cyberspace), dickwad (= jerk), digicam, eco (adj.), eco-friendly, fecker (obnoxious person), filker (= folk singer), funkadelia, fusiony, Game Boy, gay-friendly, geeked, greenwash (v.), hair band, ho-bag, hoochie (mama), infomediary, latte, macchiato (coffeee), mail bomber, minitower (computer), mommy tracker, mommy tracking, multiculti (adj., n.), mungy, murderabilia, nanobot, negaholic, negaholism, Nintendo generation, noughties (2000–2009), oppositionality, overclock (v.), paintballer, paintballing, Palmcorder, parapente (v.), power-shop (v.), Queer Nation, rug muncher, scrunchie, self-tanner, sitch (= situation), synthespian (n.), techno (adj.), threepeat (v.), unibrow (= monobrow), (computer) vaccine, wilding (n.)

Chapter 10

The World Wide Web:

1990–1999

Millions of computer users know that the *World Wide Web* (or *the Web* for short) is a system by which information is transmitted globally over the Internet, much as e-mail is. But not many users know that before 1990, the *World Wide Web* did not exist; it was created in 1990 by an English computer scientist, Sir Timothy Berners-Lee (born 1955), who also coined its name. Sir Timothy created the system by attaching hypertexts (texts that link to other texts) to the Internet. The Web revolutionized communication (*e-mail* instead of *snail mail*), business (*e-commerce, e-cash, e-money*), and online companies (*dotcoms*), and introduced users to computer language (*byte, cursor, mouse, floppy disk, PC, http, HTML, URL*). In effect, the Web brought about the electronic age that had been foreshadowed in the 1960s with the invention of the first electronic calculators. The Web spawned such new forms as *weblog, weblogger, weblogging* (contracted to *blog, blogger, blogging*), *webcam, webcast, webcasting, webliography, webmaster, webmeister, webmistress, webzine*.

The 1990s were relatively peaceful years that stimulated free expression and the creation of millions of personal, commercial, governmental, and other kinds of *websites.* The constellation of websites (images, pages, videos, etc.) accessed by computer formed a *virtual* (not real; simulated) world called *cyberspace.* In the science-fiction movie *The Matrix* (1999), the title refers to a futuristic cyberspace whose human inhabitants are unaware that the "reality" they perceive is actually simulated by machines. The combining form *cyber-* or *cybr-* was used to form many new words during the '90s and beyond, among them *Cyberia* (a science-fiction video game, with a pun on *Siberia*) and *Cyberian, cybrary* (an online library) and *cybrarian, cybercafe* (an Internet café), *cyberpet* (a virtual pet), *cybersex* (a virtual sexual encounter), and *cybershop* (a web-based shopping center). The latest development at the century's turn was the *always-on* or continuously accessible connection to the Internet by broadband, an advance promptly dubbed *Evernet*: "When telecommunications combines with the 'Evernet'—the technology that will soon allow people to get online from their watches, their cars, their toasters, or their Walkmans—, . . . everyone will be able to be connected all the time, everywhere" (Thomas L. Friedman, *New York Times,* August 10, 1999).

Another Internet-inspired combining form that became productive in the '90s was *-bot*, abstracted from *robot.* It was used to form the names of various computer programs or software that worked automatically, such as *cancelbot* (a program that cancels postings on the Internet), and *knowbot* (a program that collects information automatically from the Internet).

Most computer users conflated the Web and its

search engines (e.g., Google, Yahoo!) with the Internet, using such phrases as *going on the Internet, navigating the Internet, surfing the Internet* to describe what in effect was going online to access different websites. Some of the most popular websites of the 1990s were *Amazon.com* (books), *craigslist* (classified ads), *eBay* (auctions), and *Xanga* (blogs). Newcomers to the Internet were called *newbies,* which may have been a contraction of *new boy* (a military use) or formed after *freebie* (1925). With the proliferation of websites and blogs, a social network etiquette (*Netiquette*) developed. A number of Netiquette rules were posted on the Web by bloggers, such as the following:

> Don't write it if you wouldn't say it to a person's face.
> DON'T TYPE IN CAPS (it's like shouting).
> Use abbreviations and acronyms sparingly.
> Avoid sarcasm (most people don't appreciate it).
> Don't "flame" (send insults).
> Don't spam (send unsolicited messages).
> Respect copyrights.
> Use spellcheck.

Humor spread quickly over the Web, especially through the introduction of *emoticons* such as the *smiley face* (:), (^_^) = smile, (^o^) = laughing out loud, d(^_^)b = thumbs up, (T_T) = sad (a crying face), (-.-)Zzz = sleeping, (^_^) = cheers, hurrah. So did initialisms like *BTW* (by the way), *LOL* (laughing out loud;

lots of luck; lots of love), *OMG* (Oh My God), *IMHO* (in my humble opinion).

The success of the World Wide Web was chiefly responsible for the explosive growth of the Internet during the 1990s. Although the Internet had been known as a global computer network since the 1980s, it had been the domain of universities and governments, and it was only in the next decade that it acquired a public image. In the early years of the 1990s, the U.S. vice president, Al Gore, became associated with what he called the *information superhighway,* a network of computers for the high-speed transmission of information, which was soon identified with the Internet. Gore's public promotion of cyberspace technology became the source of the "urban legend" that he had invented the Internet, after he stated in a 1999 interview on CNN that "During my service in the United States Congress, I took the initiative in creating the Internet." It was a controversial statement, though no doubt Gore's promotion of the information superhighway helped establish the Internet during the 1990s.

The generation that came of age in the 1990s has been called the *Y generation,* since it came on the heels of *Generation X,* the group that reached adulthood in the 1980s. *Generation Yers,* sometimes called *echo boomers* (the demographic echo of the postwar baby boomers), *Millennials,* the *Net generation,* or (by shortening) *Gen Yers,* were the last generation of Americans born in the twentieth century and the first to feel more at home with personal computers and laptops than with books. Their mothers were the *soccer moms, hockey moms,* and *minivan moms* who spent half their time driving them in *minivans* or *SUV*s (*sport utility vehicles*) to soccer or hockey practice, or to ballet or music lessons. Those were the years of the Clinton presidency (1992–97, 1997–2001), during which the *European Union* (*EU*) was established, the new *euro* (€) became the official currency of the EU, *NAFTA* (*North American Free Trade Agreement*) came into being, the Cold War and the Gulf War (1990–91) were over, and new cultural trends and events were given free rein.

A national event in 1992 that sparked controversy and protests was the five hundredth anniversary of Christopher Columbus's discovery of America (he actually thought it was India, hence called the natives "Indians"). For the occasion, the word *quincentenary* (five hundredth anniversary) was resurrected by the media after having rested in peace since 1877, when it was used to commemorate the five hundredth anniversary of the death of the Bible translator John Wycliffe. Commemorative postage stamps, coins, pocket watches, and other memorabilia were issued for Columbus Day, 1992. Yet many labeled the holiday as racist. As early as October 7, 1991, *Time* magazine ignited controversy in a long article, titled "The Trouble with Columbus," in which it pointed out that "Columbus' gift was slavery to those who greeted him; his arrival set in motion the ruthless destruction, continuing at this very moment, of the natural world he entered. Genocide, ecocide, exploitation—even the notion of Columbus as a 'discoverer'—are deemed to be a form of Eurocentric theft of history from those who watched Columbus' ships drop anchor off their shores."

Another controversy of the 1990s centered on the spread of genetically modified food, crops, and organisms (*GMOs*), whose opponents coined the derogatory combining form *Franken-* in 1992. The form was abstracted from the name of (*Victor*) *Frankenstein,* the fictitious scientist who created a monster (popularly called "a Frankenstein") in Mary Shelley's 1818 novel of the same name. The combining form generated such terms as *frankenfood, frankenplants, frankenfruit,* and *frankentrees.* The entire field of genetic engineering was disparaged as *Frankenscience,* and the militant animal-rights organization *PETA* (*People for the Ethical Treatment of Animals*) decided to present every Halloween a "Frankenscience Award" to "two 'scientists' with horrendous records of drugging, isolating, and otherwise torturing animals and allow you, dear readers, the honor of telling us who makes you gag the most." Based on these coinages, the term *frankenword* was coined to designate negatively what has long been neutrally called a *blend* or (by Lewis Carroll) a *portmanteau word.* The University of Tennessee student newspaper, *The Daily Beacon,* of August 30, 1996, published this attack on such words: "Words I particularly detest are those *Frankenwords* . . . that combine two others to make one horrific abomination . . . Now we are treated to new monstrous creations, like: . . . *edutainment,* my 'favorite' *frankenword,* a cross-breeding of education and entertainment."

Franken- is a *dysphemism,* a derogatory expression used to replace a neutral one ("genetically modified"), as distinguished from a *euphemism,* a mild, roundabout, or vague expression used in place of one that is uncomfortably harsh, blunt, or offensive. A humorous example of euphemism appeared in a 1992 episode ("Kamp Krusty") of the cartoon sitcom *The Simpsons,* in an exchange between the geeky student Martin Prince Jr. and his father, Mr. Prince:

> *Mr. Prince*: We'll see you when you get back from image enhancement camp.
> *Martin Prince*: Spare me your euphemisms! It's fat camp, for Daddy's chubby little secret!

The most notorious euphemism of the 1990s was *ethnic cleansing,* first recorded in 1991 to describe the persecution, expulsion, or killing of members of various ethnic nationalities during the Bosnian war (1992–95) and other Balkan wars involved in the breakup of Yugoslavia. The term was especially egregious because it connected two essentially positive terms (*ethnic* "belonging to a people sharing a common culture, religion, language" and *cleansing* "freeing from defilement, purifying") to describe an action approaching genocide.

The terms *politically correct* and *political correctness* became controversial during the decade. Both terms, abbreviated *PC,* were used by conservatives and language purists as pejorative labels for overly liberal attitudes toward language. Thus the idea of replacing the venerable word *forefather* with *ancestor* in order to avoid the masculine *father,* or using *physically challenged* in place of *handicapped,* were condemned as creating misleading euphemisms and as "politically correct" manipulations of the mother tongue. On the liberal side, *to be PC* meant to correct centuries-old prejudices against women (sexism), nonwhites (racism), the aged (ageism), the disabled (ableism), and so on.

Political correctness was widely satirized in the media, as by making up lists of "politically correct" replacements for many common words, for example:

midget = vertically challenged
fat = horizontally challenged
body odor = nondiscretionary fragrance
dishonest = ethically disoriented
dead = living-impaired
homeless = residentially flexible

In turn, *politically incorrect* became a positive description, as in the talk show *Politically Incorrect*, hosted by the comedian Bill Maher, that ran from 1993 to to 1996 on the television channel Comedy Central.

Politically correct or not, President Bill Clinton's decision to include a provision for the *v-chip* (also spelled *V-chip*) in the Telecommunications Act he signed in 1996 was welcomed by most adult Americans. V-chips allowed parents to control and block content they didn't want their children to watch. The *v* in *v-chip* stood for *viewer* but it was commonly thought to stand for *violence*, which had been increasing on television. Since all TV programs are rated the way movies are (G, PG, MA, etc.), each rating would be encoded with a v-chip, thereby allowing parents to block specific programs or channels they deemed unsuitable for young viewers.

Others regarded the v-chip as just another fad in a decade bursting with fads. Among the most popular was the *Grunge* subculture associated with the figure of Kurt Cobain, lead singer, guitarist, and songwriter of the alternative-rock band Nirvana, who died of a drug overdose in 1994. "When did grunge become *grunge*?" was the opening line in "Grunge: A Success Story," a *New York Times* article of November 15, 1992. "How did a five-letter word meaning dirt, filth, trash become synonymous with a musical genre, a fashion statement, a pop phenomenon?" It concludes: "All subcultures speak in code; grunge is no exception. [Here's] a lexicon of grunge speak, coming soon to a high school or mall near you: WACK SLACKS: Old ripped jeans. FUZZ: Heavy wool sweaters. PLATS: Platform shoes. KICKERS: Heavy boots. . . . LAMESTAIN: Uncool person. TOM-TOM CLUB: Uncool outsiders. ROCK ON: A happy goodbye."

Other popular fads were:

gangsta rap. A style of rap music and dress developed from gang culture, noted for the fashion of *sagging* (wearing pants below the waist to expose one's underwear) and wearing baseball caps cocked to one side; *gangsta* is an alteration of *gangster*, popularized by the song "Gangsta Gangsta" (1988) by the rap group N.W.A.

Pokemon. A video-game series produced by Nintendo; the name was a romanized shortening of Japanese *poketto monsuta*, an alteration of English *Pocket Monsters*.

Tae Bo. An aerobic exercise developed from the Korean martial art *taekwondo* to promote fitness; the name was a blend of Tae(kwondo) and Bo(xing).

in-line skating. Skating on *in-line skates* (roller skates with hard rubber wheels set in a straight line, resembling the blade of an ice skate) as a sport or pastime.

Macarena. A dance performed in a rhythmic pattern of arm, hand, and hip movements in time to a fast Spanish song about a woman called in Spanish *macarena*, feminine of *macareno* "boaster, braggart."

tamagotchi. A handheld electronic toy displaying the animated image of a pet that is cared for as if it were a real pet; a digital or virtual pet. The word is from Japanese, formed from *tamago* "egg" + *uotchi* "(pocket) watch" (from English *watch*).

pogs. A game played with stacks of small discs (also called *pogs*) with the aim of winning as many pogs as possible. The name originated in Hawaii from *POG*, a brand of bottled juice made from *p*assionfruit, *o*range, and *g*uava, whose bottle caps were used to play the game in the 1930s.

Furbys (or Furbies). Small, furry electronic toy robots programmed to speak at first *Furbish*, a "language" with simple syllables and various other sounds, but gradually speaking it less and less as they "learn" to communicate in English.

Language had its fads too. An unusual vogue was the popular use of the combining form *über-* or *uber-* (from German) instead of its better-known cognates (English *over-*, Latin-origin *super-*, and Greek-origin *hyper-*). The intent seems to be to exaggerate (or possibly überexaggerate) the supposed superiority of someone or something. Examples of its use are the nouns *übergeek*, *übernerd*, *überagent*, *übermom*, and the adjectives *übercool*, *übercharged*, *überhip*. The usage was probably influenced by Nietzsche's term *Übermensch*, translated by George Bernard Shaw as *Superman* in 1907.

Several idiomatic expressions gained currency in the 1990s from actual events. One was the verbal phrase *go postal*, meaning to become suddenly enraged or violent from excessive stress, to lose control. The expression first appeared in print in the *St. Petersburg Times* of Florida on December 17, 1993: "The symposium was sponsored by the U.S. Postal Service, which has seen so many outbursts that in some circles excessive stress is known as 'going postal.' Thirty-five people have been killed in 11 post office shootings since 1983." A related noun phrase, *road rage*, meaning an uncontrollable anger expressed by a driver against other drivers on the road, became common during the decade. According to Paul McFedries's *Word Spy*, "**road rage** appeared only three times in the media from 1989 through 1993. In 1994, at least 10 stories appeared. Then things took off: In 1995, the number of stories jumped to over 200; in 1996, there were nearly 900; and in 1997, the number of stories shot up to over 2,000. **Road rage** was all the rage."

Another phrase, *mother of all* _____, was popularized after Saddam Hussein of Iraq used the phrase "the mother of all battles" (Arabic *umm al-maārik*) in

1990, in reference to the Persian Gulf War (1990–91). It is applied to anything regarded as a definitive or outstanding example of something, as in *the mother of all excuses, the mother of all search engines, the mother of all.parenting books.*

When a fact or truth is utterly obvious, staring you in the face, and yet it is ignored as if it doesn't exist, the idiom of choice to describe it is *the elephant in the room.* The original phrase was *an elephant in the living room,* used in the title of a book about alcoholism in the family, *An Elephant in the Living Room* (1984), by Jill M. Hastings and Marion H. Typpo. By the 1990s, the phrase was broadened to include any problem or situation that looms large but is neglected or goes unmentioned to avoid discomfort or difficulty, as in *The ever-weakening dollar is the elephant in the room.*

As the year 2000, popularly called *the Millennium,* drew closer, a widely perceived "bug," or programming error affecting computers, cast a dismal shadow over the immediate future of electronics. Named in 1995 the *millennium bug,* the suspected error referred to a design flaw that would record the year 2000 as 00, making it indistinguishable from the year 1900. Other names for the imminent catastrophe, whose cost to America was predicted to run into some 600 billion dollars, were the *Year 2000 Problem, Y2K,* and most terrifyingly, *Doomsday 2000.* In the event, by the time January 1, 2000, came around, most computers had managed to surmount the problem, in part because the business world, fearing the worst, had expended much time and money to fix the problem during the 1990s.

Retracing our steps to 1990, that was the year in which the venerable American Dialect Society (ADS, founded in 1889) began selecting annually the new words and phrases that best typify the year just passed. Based on its membership's nominations and votes, winners are selected and a "Word of the Year" is announced. In addition, ADS lists various categories of new words and phrases, such as "Most Likely to Succeed," "Most Useful," "Most Creative," "Most Original, "Most Euphemistic," "Most Unnecessary," and "Least Likely to Succeed." The ADS emphasizes that its selections reflect the concerns and preoccupations of the year gone by, and that the words need not be new but they are usually newly prominent. The following is a selective list of the winning terms spanning the decade of the 1990s:

1990: *Word of the Year* **Bushlips** "insincere political rhetoric" (alluding to George H. W. Bush's pledge "Read my lips: no new taxes" as he accepted the presidential nomination at the Republican National Convention in 1988; once in office, he reneged on his pledge); *Most Useful* (a tie) **technostupidity** "loss of ability through dependence on machines," and **potty parity** "equalization of toilet facilities for the sexes"; *Most Likely to Succeed* (a tie) **notebook PC** "a portable personal computer weighing 4 to 8 pounds," and **rightsizing** "adjusting the size of a working staff by laying off employees"; *Most Original* **voice merging** "the oral tradition of African-American preachers to freely use the words of others"; *Most Amazing* **bungee jumping** "the sport of jumping from a high platform with elastic cables on the feet";

Most Outrageous **politically correct** or **PC** "adhering to principles of left-wing social concern"; *Most Unnecessary* **peace dividend** "anticipated savings in military spending due to improved relations with a former enemy," as in *the peace dividend resulting from the end of the Cold War.*

1991: *Word of the Year* **mother of all** "greatest of all"; *Most Successful* **in your face** "aggressive, confrontational, flamboyant"; *Most Likely to Succeed* **rollerblade** "skate with rollers in a single row"; *Most Original* **molecular pharming** or **pharming** "genetically modifying farm animals to produce human proteins for pharmaceutical use"; *Most Amazing* **velcroid** "a person who sticks like Velcro to the President, especially for photo opportunities."

1992: *Word of the Year* **Not!** "expression of disagreement" (as in *I'm kidding. Not!*); *Most Likely to Succeed* **snail mail** or **s-mail** "mail that is physically delivered, as opposed to e-mail"; *Most Original* **Franken-** "genetically altered"; *Most Outrageous* **ethnic cleansing** "purging of ethnic minorities"; *Most Amazing* **Munchausen's syndrome by proxy** "illness fabricated to evoke sympathy for the caregiver"; *Most Useful* **grunge** "a style of clothing (e.g., bleached and ripped jeans)"; *Most Unnecessary* **gender feminism** "belief that sex roles are social, not biological."

1993: *Word of the Year* **information superhighway** (see above); *Most Likely to Succeed* **quotative** *like,* used with a form of the verb *be* to indicate speech or thought (as in *She was, like, Oh my God!*); *Most Useful* **thing** premodified by a noun, e.g. "a Chicago thing"; *Most Amazing* **cybersex** "sexual stimulation by computer"; *Most*

Imaginative **McJob** "a generic unstimulating, low-paying job"; *Most Euphemistic* **street builder** "a homeless person who constructs a shanty"; *Most Outrageous* **whirlpooling** "assault of a female by a male group in a swimming pool"; *Most Unnecessary* **mosaic culture** "a multicultural society."

1994: *Word of the Year* (a tie) **cyber** "pertaining to computers and electronic communication," and **morph** "to change form"; *Most Trendy* **dress down day** or **casual day** "a workday when employees are allowed to dress casually"; *Most Euphemistic* **challenged,** indicating an undesirable or unappealing condition (as in *morally challenged*); *Most Promising* **Infobahn** "the Internet."

1995: *Word of the Year* **World Wide Web** (see above); *Most Likely to Succeed* **World Wide Web** and its variants (**the Web, WWW**, etc.); *Most Useful* **E.Q.** (for **Emotional Quotient**) "the ability to manage one's emotions, seen as a factor in achievement"; *Most Original* **go postal** "to act irrationally, often violently, from stress at work"; *Most Outrageous* **starter marriage** "a first marriage not expected to be the last (akin to *starter home*)."

1996: *Word of the Year* **mom** (as in **soccer mom, single mom**), the newly significant type of voter; *Most Likely to Succeed* **drive-by**, designating brief visits or hospital stays (as in *drive-by mastectomy*); *Most Useful* **dot,** used instead of *period* in e-mail and URL addresses; *Most Original* **prebuttal** "preemptive rebuttal; quick response to a political adversary"; *Most Euphemistic* (a tie) **urban**

camping "living homeless in a city," and **food insecure**, said of a country where people are starving; *Most Controversial* **Ebonics** "African-American Vernacular English"; *Most Unnecessary* **Mexican hustle** "the Macarena" (a misnomer).

1997: *Word of the Year* **millennium bug** (see above); *Most Likely to Succeed* **DVD** (*Digital Video Disk*), optical disk technology expected to replace CDs; *Most Useful* (a tie) **-[r]azzi** "an aggressive pursuer" (as in *stalkerazzi*), and the derisive interjection **duh,** used to express another's ignorance or stupidity; *Most Original* **prairie dogging** "popping one's head above an office cubicle out of curiosity."

1998: *Word of the Year* **e-** (for *electronic*), newly productive prefix, as in *e-business, e-commerce, e-tailing* (retailing on the Internet); *Most Useful* and *Most Likely to Succeed* **e-**; *Most Euphemistic* **senior moment** "a momentary lapse of memory by a senior citizen"; *Most Original* **multislacking** "playing at the computer when one should be working"; *Least Likely to Succeed* **compfusion** "confusion over computers."

1999: *Word of the Year* **Y2K** "the year 2000"; *Most Useful* and *Most Likely to Succeed* **dot-com** "a company doing business on the Web"; *Most Original* **cybersquat** "to register a Web address intending to sell it at a profit"; *Most Euphemistic* **compassionate conservative,** political label of presidential candidate George W. Bush; *Most Outrageous* **humanitarian intervention** "military force used for humanitarian purposes."

A Selection of New Words of the 1990–1999 Decade

1990

applet, archaeal, archaeon, bicurious, caipiroska (cocktail),
cereologist, cringeworthy, digitbox, downshifter, drag and
drop, DWEM (Dead White European Male), e- (electronic),
emoticon, feminazi, gangsta rap, gayby boom (= babies raised
by gays), gengineer (v.), greenwash (n.), greenwashing, happy-
clappy, hyperlinking, Islamofascism, -istan, jibab, killfile (v.),
lesbigay (adj., n.), line dance (v.), low-five (v.), malware,
martial artistry, Merkin (= American), messager,
microlending, Mijito, mitumba, morphing, mountain bike
(v.), nanite (= nanorobot), nanorobot, new jack (swing music),
new jill swing, noisecore (music), Nostraticist, nunchuck (v.),
nutraceutical (adj.), nymphomanic (n., adj.), out (v.), outing,
perestroikan (n., adj.), Perm Five (UN Security Council
members), pharm, photo CD, picon, polyamorous, portobello,
props, shout-out, skeeve (sleazy person), slaphead,
smackdown, soulstress, star 69 (v., n. = call return service),
technostupidity, teledildonics, World Wide Web

1991

abdominoplasty, babelicious, bankassurance, bankassurer,
bitch-slap (v.), boardercross (snowboarding), carjacking,
channel-grazer, crowd-surf (v.), Cyberia, Cyberian, cybersex,

cybrarian, desk rage, docusoap, down-low (adj.), Energizer Bunny, ethnic cleansing, FAQ (frequently asked questions), filk (v., = folk), GMO (genetically modified organism), grunger, Gulf War syndrome, information fatigue, ka-ching (v.), loungecore (dance music), mailmerge (v.), Mercosur (common market), microbusiness, microkernel (computer), microlender, mijo (= mi hijo), morph (n.), mother of all, muxed (= multiplexed), netcast (v.), not! (negating a previous statement), nu skool (music), overclocking, parascend (v.), permaculturist, PGP (pretty good privacy), pharming, phytoremediation, postcoloniality, psychedelic trance (music), queercore (music), riffage, sampladelic, sarcopenia, satphone, Sensex, shoegazer, shoegazing, skeeved, slowcore (music), SoHo (Small office, Home office), soul patch, spam (v.), telecottaging, tighty-whities, UNSCOM (UN Special Commission), velcroid, WMD (weapon of mass destruction)

1992

biodiesel, biodiversity, celly (= cell phone), chemokine, Clintonite, Clintonomics, cyber (adj.), cyberwar, cypherpunk, dandiya (stick dancing), digerati, dilbert (v.), drive-by (= hurried), drum and bass (dance music), dumbsizing, eatertainment, e-business, emocore (music), ethnic cleanser, euro, feck (interj.), Franken-, Generation Y, glass wall, GM (genetically modified), grrrl, grunge (fashion), henna tattooing, http (hypertext transfer protocol), infinity pool, junglist, luppie (= lesbian urban professional), magnetar (neutron star), mini-putt, mixmastered (adj.), Munchausen syndrome by proxy, NAFTA, nannycam, nanobacterium, netcast (n.), netizen (= Internet citizen), ninja (v.), off-message, on-message, down-low (= closet homosexuality), otaku, PC (= political correctness), P2P (adj., = peer-to-peer), permaculturalist, polyamorist, polyamory, photoshop (v.), pressé (fruit juice), pretexting, proplyd (protoplanetary disc), rainbow nation, riot girl, sadcore (music), same-sex (= homosexual), s-mail, smartifact, snail mail, squoval (square-oval fingernail), stylometrician, superwaif, surf (the Internet), technoshaman, technoshamanism, turntablist, URL (Uniform Resource Locator), v-mail (= video mail), WWW or www (World Wide Web)

1993

alpha geek, bird flu, -bot, bumsters, cancelbot, chick lit, Clipper chip, commentariat, cyberpet, cybershop (v.), cybrary (n.), dumbsize (v.), DVD (digital video disk), dwarf planet, e-commerce, emo (= emocore), e-money, European Union (EU), euro-wasp, extropian, fen-phen, geeksville, genderquake, go postal, home page, HTML (Hypertext Markup Language), information superhighway, Internot (one refusing to use the Internet), irritainment, janky (bad,

untrustworthy), jukebox musical, limoncelle, mail-bomb
(v.), media wasp, microdermabrasion, mosaic culture,
mouse potato, mwah-mwah (air kisses), name and shame
(v.), nanobacterial, Netspeak, overclocker, paperazzi
(= newspaper reporters), paramotor, pepper-spray (v.),
permatemp, pescatorian, pogs (game), Power Ranger,
samplist, snowblading, talkoff, trip hop, trip hopper,
v-chip, virtual pet, weblog, weblogger, weblogging,
web site/website, whirlpooling

1994

agroterrorism, artilect, bar-code hairstyle, Benjamin
(= Benji), bioinformaticist, Botox (v.), bootylicious, channel-
hopping (adj.), copicide, cyber-, cybercafé, cybershop (n.),
dot-com/dotcom (n.), e-cash, e-zine, flexecutive, Infobahn,
kitesurfer, knowbot, mattifying (adj.), Megan's Law,
metrosexual (n., adj.), middle-of-the-roadness, mullet
(hair style), Netlag, Netscape, nitrophobic, outplant (n.),
OxyContin, paladar, paramotoring, phen-fen, phytonutrient,
plutino, polyamorist, polyamory, qubit, ramidus, sampladelia,
sandboard (v.), screenager, slapheaded, slapheadedness, spam
(v.), spammer, spamming, spyware, starter marriage,
strollerobics, supersize (v.), surgiholic, sylvanshine, Tae Bo,
telnetable (adj.), text message (v.), thumb candy, Toronto
blessing, trip hop, wakeboard (v.), wakeboarding, webmaster,

webmeister, webmistress, webzine, Xenical, zorse (zebra-horse hybrid)

1995

advertecture, agrimation, backronym (reverse acronym), begathon, CGI Joe (average computer programmer), crunk (adj.), cyberscriber, cybersquatter, disattention, disintermediation, e-tailer, e-tailing, e-ticket, e-ticketing, euro note, extranet, genomicist, globitarian, hacktivist, kitesurfing, leptin, Lollywood (Lahore film industry), luser (stupid computer user, blend of loser and user), Macarena, macdink (v.), meatspace (the physical world), Milf/MILF (sexy mature woman), militician, netcaster, netcasting, picture messaging, prebiotic, Propecia, proteome, racino (= racetrack casino), slanguist, slurvian (slurred English, e.g., hafta, gonna), strollerobics, webcam, webcast (n., v.), webcasting, webliography, wiki, wordfact

---

1996

air guitar, alcopop, always-on, anecdata, bashment, bioinformatician, cheminformatics, clickstream, cybersquatting, Dogme/Dogma, dot-com/dotcom (v.), E-day (= Euro-day), the elephant in the room, entertoyment, EQ (= emotional quotient), face time, flame (e-mail insult), gastroporn, granny bank, grass ceiling, hacktivism, kiteboard, kiteboarding, kwaito, logophilia, mattifier, microbrowser, mini-me, minivan mom, mixy-matchy, modelizer, mountainboard, mountainboarder, mountainboarding, MP3, nutraceutical (n.), office (v.), Padanian (n., adj.), phish, phishing, Mexican hustle, prebuttal, psy-trance (= psychedelic trance), roofie (= Rohypnol), scratchiti, senior moment, shoulder-surfing, smokesploitation, spamdexing, stalkerazzi, subprime (adj.), Talibanization, thugged out, tipping point, turntablism, urban camping, Viagra, the Web, W3, webcaster, webisode (= web episode)

1997

affluenza, air rage, angst bunny, Appletini (martini), bigorexic (adj., n.), blamestorming, body dysmorphic disorder (BDD), careware (software benefiting charity), charityware, clap skate, corrections cocktail, disintermediation, dot-commer, e-learning, e-print, evo-devo (= evolutionary-developmental), exit bag, explornography, fanfic (= fan fiction), fleshwriter, Florida flambé, gastronaut, goodware (= careware), handheld (n.), helpware (= careware), innernet, Internetese, jitterati (= coffee addict), MAD (millennial anxiety disorder), mattify, m-commerce, megalogue (= large-scale dialogue), Muggle, orthorexia, orthorexic (n., adj.), pathopoeic, pharmer, phone family, piconet, push poll (designed to promote candidate), robo-roach, shockumentary, shruggism, shruggist, smackdown, snowboardcross, spamouflage, subvertisement, subvertising (= subverted advertising), surfcaster, teledildonics, UCE (unsolicited commercial e-mail), Web rage, work rage

---

1998

BioSteel, birdosaur, Bluetooth, Cablinasian (Caucasian, Black, Indian, Asian), coffeezilla, coolhunter, cosleeping, cybersquat, dilberted, dittohead, dark energy, e-book, egosurfing, eigenface, e-learning, e-reader, e-tail (= electronic retail), e-tailer, facebase, flexplace, fluffragette, Furby, Google (v.), greenwash (v.), hacktivist, Japanimation, kiteboard (v.), kiteboarder, mesotherapy, millennium bug, milly (= millennium), mousetrapping, nanny bubble, Nexus Generation, off-road skating, photophoresis, portal site, proteomics, rumorazzi, shagadelic, sneakernet, snowblader, spamouflage, spintronic, spintronics, taikonaut, Talibanize, Talibanized, Talibanization, Tamagotchi (virtual pet), techno-strike, treeware, über-, upsell (v.), voice novel, WAP (wireless application protocol), webinar, WI-FI (adj., n.), xenotransplant, Yogalates (trademark Yogilates), yuppie puppy (= second-generation yuppie), zinester (zine writer), zombie (computer)

1999

alpha mom, arm candy, biopiracy, bird dog, bitlegging (digital bootlegging), blast fax, bling (n, adj.), blog (n., v.), blogger, blogging, brownfield, B2B (= business-to-business), bubble tea, carry tax, chip graffiti, compcierge, completist, cyberpiracy, cyberpirate, data fast, day trade (v.), day trader, day trading, debt porn, dog food (v.), dollarize, dread merchant, Evernet, e-wallet, farmageddon, fiscalamity, Fraud-U-Net (adj.), genericide, green bullet, i-biology, ICU psychosis, identity theft, informavore, Internet time, job lock, luppie (= Latino urban professional), mathlete, me-moir, microbrowser, microcinema, microsleep, millionerd, multi-skilling, mung (n, v., mash until no good), optionaire, page-jack (v.), permanent fresh (adj.), pie (v.), Pokemania, rage rage, rumortism, shilling/shill bidding, smartsizing, sneaker millionaire, snortometer, soccerplex, stealth tower, teleworkaholic, transgenic, trophy tree, virtual advertising, weather tourism, weather tourist, webmail, Webology, Y2K

Chapter 11

The Third Millennium:

2000–2009

"What are we going to call the decade after the decade of the Nineties?" asked the language maven William Safire in his book *Quoth the Maven* (1993). He was referring to the decade from 2000 to 2009, and it was a challenging question. After all, who can remember what the decade from 1900 to 1909 was called, if anything? From 1910 onward people casually talked of "the '10s," "the '20s," "the '30s," and so on. But the first decade of the new century was like a foundling, nameless.

Many rose to the challenge. "The *Naughties* was suggested by forty readers," reported Mr. Safire, " . . . but I am turning this down because of the archness of the double meaning." (The pun on *Naughty*, as in the *Naughty Nineties*, could have been avoided by opting for the variant spelling *Noughties*; indeed the British, according to the *OED*, promptly adopted the variant.) Other proposed names that failed to gain approval included the *Aughties*, the *Ohs*, and the *Double-O's*. Wikipedia, the Web-based free encyclopedia, also lists *double-aughts*, *nils* and *nillies*, *2Ks*, and *ozies*.

Alas, the decade is almost over without a name, which suggests that there was no need to name it in the first place. As for naming each year of the decade,

Mr. Safire recommended using *oh*, as in *twenty oh six* for 2006, which followed nicely the informal *nineteen oh six* for 1906 of the previous century. (The formal name was *nineteen hundred and six*.) So far, it turns out that current usage favors the formal *two thousand and six* or *two thousand six*. As to what the year 2020 will be called—*two thousand twenty* or simply *twenty twenty*, like the TV show—it seems pretty certain that *twenty twenty* will prevail. Already websites like *2020 technology, twenty twenty wines, 2020 summer Olympics,* and *2020 companies* are crowding the Internet.

The first new word to make headlines in 2000 was actually an obscure word, *chad,* meaning the small piece of paper removed from a punched card or tape. The *OED* records the word since 1959 and declares it "origin unknown." Until the presidential election of 2000, in which George W. Bush and Al Gore were in a dead heat, chads were of no consequence beyond their occasional use as confetti. But when it transpired that the outcome of the election hinged on a bunch of partially attached chads, of the word gained instant notoriety. As the state of Florida's twenty-five electoral votes were in the balance, requiring a manual recount of the ballots, it was found that many of the state's punch-card ballots were incompletely punched. The chads hanging from those ballots were then placed into four categories, namely: *hanging chads,* those barely attached, dangling by one corner; *swinging chads,* those attached at two corners, like a door on a hinge; *tri-chads,* those attached at three corners; and *dimpled* or *pregnant chads,* those fully attached but bearing a swollen spot as evidence that they were intended to be punched through. The manual recount was ultimately stopped by the Supreme Court, a decision that handed the presidency to George W. Bush.

The 2000 presidential election also popularized the terms *red state* and *blue state* for states whose voters belonged largely to the Republican Party (red) and the Democratic Party (blue). The terms were derived from the color scheme of the maps shown on television and in some newspapers during the election campaign. Since 2000 the two terms have been extended in use: *red state* for any state regarded as mainly Republican or conservative, and *blue state* for any state regarded as mainly Democratic or liberal. Since red and blue combine to form purple, the term *purple state* was coined for any state in which no candidate has a clear-cut majority among voters. Such states have been called *battleground states* since the 1960s or, since 1980, *swing states.*

The first year of the new decade, century, and millennium was consumed with *blogs* (*weblogs*), websites serving up personal commentaries, editorials, or journals, as well as with *Webology* (the study of the World Wide Web) and *Webliography* (lists of links to subjects or themes found on the Web, on the model of *bibliography*). So much space was given to blogs that a whole new sphere arose in cyberspace, the *blogosphere,* a collective name for the world of blogs, including their writers, readers, and the multitude of subjects they tackled. The adjective *bloggy* ("of blogs, like a blog") became widespread. Among the newer blogs were *audioblogs* (blogs with links to audio files); *vlogs* (video blogs), consisting mostly of videos presented by *vloggers*; *moblogs* (mobile blogs), which cover postings from cell phones; and, most disturbingly, *flogs* (fake blogs), blogs pretending to be a person's work but in reality produced by marketers, advertisers, and public-relations agents *flogging* products, businesses, and organizations.

A visual version of blogging is *lifecasting*, the broadcasting of daily routines and events in a person's life over the Internet by means of wearable computers and webcams. Another pastime facilitated by the Internet is *geocaching*, a treasure-hunting game in which a trinket or other item (called a *geocache*) is hidden in a waterproof container anywhere in the world, to be found through the Global Positioning System (GPS) by means of coordinates posted on a website. Probably the most popular game of the decade was the number puzzle *sudoku*, whose objective is to fill a nine-by-nine-box grid with the numbers 1 to 9 so that every number appears only once in each column, each row, and each of the nine three-by-three blocks or subdivisions. The game got its name from Japanese, in which it was contracted from the phrase *su*(uji wa) *doku*(shin ni kagiru), "the digits are limited to a single occurrence." Another number puzzle popularized in 2008 was *KenKen* (from Japanese *ken* "cleverness," *ken ken* "cleverness squared"), which requires basic arithmetic skills (addition, subtraction, multiplication, division) for its solution.

New developments on the Internet were the *dotbams*, or online branches or divisions of regular companies or businesses. The term *dotbam* was modeled on the *dotcom* of the 1990s, but formed from *dot* + *bam*, abbreviation of *bricks-and-mortar*. The latter term inspired the coinage of *clicks-and-mortar*, meaning a dotbam or its activities. Perhaps a more productive term to capture the Internet was *wiki*, meaning a web page or collection of web pages designed to enable anyone who accesses it to contribute or modify its content. The word derived from the first website of this kind, *WikiWikiWeb* (1995), formed from Hawaiian *wikiwiki* "quick, quick" (from English *quickie*). Internet users have become familiar with such derivative terms (and websites) as *Wikipedia* (an editable online encyclopedia), *Wiktionary* (an editable online dictionary), *wikiNode* (an editable site that links wikis), and *wikiHow* (an editable how-to manual).

Cybercrimes by computer hackers expanded in the 2000s. Aside from the regular *malware* (viruses, worms, trojan horses), there were crimes like *webjacking*, which involved the theft of a website or its files by redirecting them to a fraudulent site. To *webjack* a business is to steal its customers. Another illegal activity was *mousetrapping*, in which a visitor is trapped at a website and assaulted by unsolicited pop-up ads. *Mousetrappers* typically ensnare consumers by registering a website with the misspelled name of a celebrity. A subset of mousetrapping is *page-jacking*, where hackers redirect or reset a user's home page to use it fraudulently. Then there is the *zombie computer* (or just *zombie*), a standard computer that a hacker has furtively infected with malware and uses it to perform fraudulent or malicious tasks by remote control.

A very large computer worm infecting the Microsoft Windows operating systems of millions of computers in hundreds of countries surfaced in late 2008. It was called *Conficker* and nicknamed *Downup* and *Kido*. The worm's name has been described as an alteration of the word "configure" or of "trafficconverter," but its exact origin is unknown.

Still, progress in computer and Internet technology moved apace, led by the launching in 2000 of the digital media player *iTunes* and in 2001 of the digital audio player *iPod*, followed in 2003 by the free Internet telephony service *Skype*, the social networking websites *MySpace* and *Facebook* in 2003 and 2004, the photo-and-video-sharing website *Flickr* in 2004, the video-sharing website *YouTube* in 2005, and the social networking and blogging website *Twitter* in 2006. The decade also saw the introduction of interactive whiteboards called *smartboards* into schools, and the widespread use of *podcasts*, digital recordings of a radio or other broadcast available on the Internet for downloading to a portable media player. The word was formed from (*i*)*Pod* + (*broad*)*cast*, and used as a verb (*How to podcast*) or as a noun or adjective *podcasting*, as in *podcasting in education* and *podcasting tools*. In 2007, the online retailer Amazon.com launched the *Kindle e-reader*, which made electronic books widely accessible. But unlike *p-books* (print books), which are the permanent property of purchasers, *e-books* remain under the control of publishers, who may at will remove, recall, change, or delete any of their books.

Internet-based communication became collectively

known as *social media,* which included *social network* sites (e.g., *Facebook, MySpace, LinkedIn, XING*), *news aggregators* (e.g., *Digg* and *Reddit*), *social bookmarks* (e.g., *Delicious, StumbleUpon*), *knowledge-sharing* sites (e.g., *Wikipedia, Yahoo Answers, Google Earth*), *microblogs/microblogging* (e.g., *Twitter, identi.ca, laconi.ca*), and photo-and-video-sharing sites like *YouTube* and *Flickr.* The common denominator of all these sites is that much of their content is initiated by individuals who use the Internet to express themselves. In countries like China, Iran, Syria, and others where the government blocks access to certain websites, a free software called *Freegate* is widely used by *hacktivists* (1995) to break into the banned sites.

Other Internet innovations were the introduction by Google in 2007 of the free webmail service *Gmail* (called *Google Mail* in Great Britain), and the launching by Microsoft in 2009 of the search engine *Bing.* But probably the most common method of communication during the decade was *texting* or *text messaging,* sending short (maximum 160 characters) messages from cell phones or other digital devices like *smartphones* (iPhone, BlackBerry, Palm Pre, etc.). "The obvious appeal of texting is its speed. There is, as it happens, a Ten Commandments of texting, as laid down by one Norman Silver, the author of *Laugh Out Loud :-D.* The fourth of these commandments reads, 'u shall b prepard @ all times 2 tXt & 2 recv'" (Louis Menand, "Thumbspeak," *New Yorker,* October 20, 2008). Texting sexually explicit messages spawned the portmanteau word *sexting,* as in the *USA Today* headline

(March 11, 2009) "Teens Caught 'Sexting' Face Porn Charges."

Another trend was converting the names of websites into verbs. Thus the name of the search engine Google was changed in 2002 to the verb *google,* defined in the *Oxford English Dictionary* as "*intr.* To use the Google search engine to find information on the Internet. *trans.* To search for information about (a person or thing) using the Google search engine." Sometimes the trend went beyond functional change, as in the case of the social networking site Twitter, whose name was turned into the verb *tweet,* as in this letter by U.S. senator Claire McCaskill in the May 10, 2009, Sunday *Times* magazine: "I'd like to explain why I tweet.... First, through Twitter, I am able to post information daily on a public bulletin board about serious policy issues.... Second, tweeting is a discipline that keeps me connected." Messages sent through Twitter are also known as *tweets,* each tweet limited to 140 characters, as in "In Iran, tweets vs. bullets" (*New York Times,* June 18, 2009). Other words derived from Twitter include *Twitterer* (Twitter user), *twitterati* (Twitterers as a group, after *glitterati* and *literati*), and *tweetup* (a meeting of Twitterers).

The *genericization* of brand names like Kleenex and Xerox—that is, their being turned into common nouns or verbs (*a kleenex, to xerox*)—was until recently thought to be the death knell for a trademark. But *genericide,* as this process has been called, was, to the surprise of trademark lawyers, encouraged during this decade. The chief executive of the search engine *Bing,* for example, expressed the hope that some day "people will 'bing' a new restaurant to find its address or 'bing' a new job applicant for telling events in his past" (*New York Times*, July 19, 2009). And the news aggregator website *Digg.com* freely uses its name in lowercase (*digg*), as a verb (*Did you digg it?*), as a present participle (*digging*), and even in a newly formed past tense (*dugg*). The reason for this change in thinking is the speed with which dot-com firms rise and disappear, making market share all-important in the Internet age, even at the cost of allowing one's brand name to become generic.

For most Americans, the defining word of the decade was *9/11* or *9-11*, pronounced "nine eleven," referring to the September 11, 2001, suicide attacks on the United States by al Qaeda terrorists that killed nearly three thousand people. The word *9/11* was distinguished from the similar but much older *911* (for the national telephone emergency number) in two ways: orthographically, the telephone number has no dividing slash or hyphen, and phonetically, it is pronounced "nine one one." The 9/11 attacks catapulted al Qaeda (a pan-Islamic terrorist group whose name means "the Base" in Arabic) and the name of its founder, Osama bin Laden, into instant infamy. Within days of the attack, President George W. Bush proclaimed a *war on terror*, aimed at *Islamofascists* everywhere, not only al Qaeda, but other *jihadist* groups like the *Taliban*, *Hezbollah*, and *Hamas*. Some months later, President Bush labeled governments that aided terrorism as forming an *axis of evil*, naming specifically Iran, Iraq, and North Korea. On the assumption that Iraq concealed *WMD*s (weapons of mass destruction), which included biological and chemical weapons, the United States invaded Iraq in 2003. Using a military technique of *shock and awe,* American forces used intensive aerial bombing to overwhelm Iraqi defenses. But since no WMDs were ever found in Iraq, the Iraq War proved to be one of the most unpopular of U.S. wars. Meanwhile, suspected terrorists were transported to foreign countries for detention and interrogation in what was known as *rendition* or *extraordinary rendition,* a controversial policy that sometimes exposed detainees to *waterboarding,* an interrogation technique in which the subject is immobilized on his back as water is poured over the face, causing him to experience the symptoms of drowning. Waterboarding was just one of the euphemistically called *enhanced interrogation techniques* developed by the government's *SERE* (*Survival, Evasion, Resistance, Escape*) training program. Meanwhile *ground zero,* the site of New York's World Trade Towers after they collapsed on 9/11, has become a symbol and memorial of the most catastrophic act of terror perpetrated in U.S. history.

With the election in 2009 of Barack Obama to the presidency, *Obamamania* and *Obamaphoria* swept the nation, and the new generation of his supporters became known as the *O Generation.* The editors of the online magazine *Slate* even made up a slate of Barack Obama–based terms, which were published under the title *Obamamania! The English Language, Barackafied.* Included among the terms were such concoctions as *Baractogenerian* (an over-twenty Obama supporter), *Baracketry* (the science of Barack design, development, and flight), *Barackintosh* (a computer that is highly likely to identify its owner as an Obama supporter), *Obamage* (Obama homage), *Obamanation* (the United States the day after Obama's inauguration), *Obamazon* (a female Obama supporter), *Obamatopia*, and 128 pages more of the same.

The country hoped that the Obama administration would reverse the *market meltdown* that began in late 2008 due to risky *subprime* loans on mortgages that led to a *credit crunch*, necessitating the *bailout* of failing companies and banks and the need for *gas-sippers* as opposed to *gas-guzzlers*, among other remedies. The credit crunch, which was a sharp reduction in the availability of loans, was also referred to as the *credit squeeze*, the *credit crisis*, and the *finance crunch*.

The financial crisis deepened quickly into a major recession that by late 2008 spread to all the continents. On the model of the Great Depression, it became known as the *Great Recession*. "We are in uncertain times as the Great Recession of 2008 is . . . looking to be the longest and by some measures the worst since WWII" (Thomas Lee, *Smart Money*, December 22, 2008).

The public was angst-ridden with news about *toxic assets* that no one wanted, about *credit default swaps* (*CDS*), about proposals for a *futarchy* (a government by prediction markets), and about fashionable *frugalistas* and *recessionistas* (frugal but stylish shoppers). Some turned to hosting or attending *gold parties* to make cash from jewelry, others opted for *saver's credit* to trim their federal income tax, still others got into *Internet-based bartering*. To reduce stress, many took to alternative therapies like *Feldenkrais* (a method that builds on efficiency of movement), *Chigong* or *Qigong* (similar to *tai chi*), or *Reiki* (spreading healing energy by hand movement). Others crossed their fingers and prayed for an economic *game-changer*. But most rested their hopes on *Obamanomics,* the new economic policies of the Obama administration (2009–2013).

The latter was the latest incarnation of the suffix *-(o)nomics* (remember *Nixonomics* and *Reaganomics*?), triggered by the popularity of *freakonomics,* a term coined by Steven D. Levitt and Stephen J. Dubner in a 2005 book about the application of economic theory to just about everything. The term led to a spate of words like *womenomics, scroogeenomics, titlenomics,* and *slackonomics.* There was also a striking revival of the old combining form *-gate* (see Chapter 8), broadened to mean any scandal involving politics or politicians, as in *Blagojevichgate* (Illinois governor Rod Blagojevich), *Spitzergate* (New York governor Eliot Spitzer), *Palingate* (Alaska governor Sarah Palin), *wardrobegate* (about Governor Palin's expensive wardrobe), *troopergate* (about Alaska state trooper Mike Wooten). Another usage development was the proliferation of clipped words, popularly called *abbrevs,* especially among teenagers, such as *awk* (for *awkward*), *bellig* (for *belligerent*), *brill* (for *brilliant*), *drams* (for *dramatics*), *pleas* (for *pleasure*), *probs* (for *probably*), *whatev* (for *whatever*), and *the yoozh* (for *the usual*).

Other new words and phrases that gained attention during the decade include:

boomeranger [2001]. An adult offspring who returns home after college to live with his baby-boomer parents. "They go by many different names: 'boomerangers,' 'nesters,' 'homebounders,' 'twixters'—you name it" (Elina Furman, *The Boomeranger in the Basement*, 2005).

eco-chic, n. [2009]. A combination of trendiness and environmentalism; ecological chic. —**adj.** Combining trendiness and environmentalism; ecologically chic. "The Eco-Chic Living Guide to Be More Green" (*Marie Claire*, June 19, 2009).

eventize, v.t. [2004]. To turn (products or services) into an event in order to promote and market them. "A première lets the marketing and publicity teams join in a final effort to 'eventize' a film, to move it to the top of the nation's long to-do list" (*New Yorker*, January 19, 2009).

fat tail [2001]. In finance, an abnormal accumulation of catastrophic events, such as credit crunches and stock market crashes. "But what about the *fat tail*? This is another way of asking 'How come all you geniuses didn't realize the risk you were running?'" (William Safire, *New York Times Magazine*, February 5, 2009).

green job [2007]. A job related to improvements in environmental quality, such as weatherizing buildings or installing solar panels. "The new Green Jobs Act is a bill that will help train workers in environmental labor" (NPR, July 18, 2007).

hackable [2006]. (Of an electronic program or device) capable of being modified. "The Chumby is Internet-connected . . . and is extremely hackable" (Rob Walker, *New York Times Magazine*, June 22, 2008).

hip-hop hug [2003]. A combined handshake and one-armed hug between two males. "The hip-hop hug a.k.a. the *man hug* and the *hetero hug*. Shake with right hand and hug with left, two slaps on the back" (*Time*, February 23, 2009).

Madoff, v.t. [2009]. To swindle, especially in an elaborate investment fraud like that perpetrated by Bernard L. Madoff between the early 1990s and 2008. "Please tell us somebody gets Madoffed" (*Time*, February 23, 2009). "NYT must-read on how big polluters 'Madoffed' the American people" (Luis Hastres, *1Sky*, April 24, 2009).

snowclone [2004] A formulaic cliché. "'China is the new Japan.' 'Much ado about ballroom dancing.' When you read phrases like these in a newspaper, you've stumbled across a particular kind of cliché: the snowclone. Snowclones spring from a rich diversity of sources, from Shakespeare ('To X or not to X?') to *Star Trek* ('It's X, but not as we know it') ..." (*New Scientist*, November 18, 2006).

As we did in the preceding chapter, we turn to the American Dialect Society's Words of the Year selections for the present decade. The ADS has been choosing Words of the Year since 1990. Not just *the* Word of the Year, but other new or notable terms in various categories, such as Most Useful, Most Creative, Most Likely to Succeed, Most Euphemistic, Most Outrageous, Most Unnecessary, and Least Likely to Succeed. The following is a selective list of the Words of the Year for the present decade:

2000: *Word of the Year* **chad** "a small scrap of paper punched from a ballot"; *Most Useful* **civil union** "a legal same-sex marriage"; *Most Creative* **dot bomb** "a failed dotcom"; *Most Likely to Succeed* **muggle** "a banal, unimaginative person" (after the ordinary *Muggles* in the Harry Potter books); *Most Euphemistic* **courtesy call** "an uninvited call from a telemarketer"; *Most Outrageous* **wall humping** "rubbing one's pants pocket against a scanner that reads security cards to avoid the inconvenience of removing the card from one's pocket"; *Most Unnecessary* **sudden loss of wealth syndrome** "feelings of shame, guilt, and humiliation resulting from sudden impoverishment"; *Least Likely to Succeed* **kablokeys** "the dickens, the devil (as in *It scared the kablokeys out of me*)."

2001: *Word of the Year* **9-11** or **9/11** "the terrorist attacks of September 11, 2001"; *Most Useful* (a tie) **facial profiling** "identification of suspects by videotaping their faces," and **second-hand speech** "overheard cell-phone conversation in public places"; *Most Creative* **shuicide/ shoeicide bomber** "terrorist with a bomb in his shoe"; *Most Likely to Succeed* **9-11** or **9/11** (same as Word of the Year); *Most Euphemistic* **daisy cutter** "a large bomb that explodes a few feet above the ground"; *Most Outrageous* **assoline** "methane used as a fuel"; *Most Unnecessary* **impeachment nostalgia** "a longing for superficial news (as those of the Clinton era)."

2002: *Word of the Year* **weapons of mass destruction** or **WMD** (sought for in Iraq); *Most Useful* **google** (verb) "to search the Web for information using the Google search engine"; *Most Creative* **Iraqnophobia** "strong fear of Iraq" (a pun on *arachnophobia*); *Most*

Likely to Succeed **blog** (from *weblog*) "a website of personal events, comments, and links"; *Most Euphemistic* **regime change** "forced change in leadership."

2003: *Word of the Year* **metrosexual** "a fashion-conscious heterosexual male"; *Most Useful* **flexitarian** "a vegetarian who occasionally eats meat"; *Most Creative* **freegan** "a person who eats only what can be got for free"; *Most Likely to Succeed* **SARS** "a viral disease, Severe Acute Respiratory Syndrome"; *Most Euphemistic* **preemptive self-defense** "an attack made before a possible enemy attack"; *Most Unnecessary* **Freedom** (replacing "French" in *French fries*, etc.); *Least Likely to Succeed* **tomacco** "a poisonous hybrid of tomato and tobacco." Other candidates included **embed** "to place journalists with troops or a political campaign," the combining form **-shoring** "indicating the location of jobs or businesses, as in *nearshoring*, moving them to Canada," **text**, v. "to send a text message," and **tanorexia** "the condition of being addicted to tanning."

2004: *Word of the Year* **red/blue/purple states** "(red) states favoring conservative Republicans/(blue) states favoring liberal Democrats/(purple) states undecided"; *Most Useful* **phish** "to induce someone to reveal private information by means of deceptive e-mail"; *Most Creative* **pajamahadeen** "bloggers in their bedclothes who challenge and fact-check traditional media" (a blend of *pajama* and *mujahideen*); *Most Likely to Succeed* **red/blue/purple states** (same as Word of the Year); *Most Euphemistic* **badly sourced** "false"; *Most Unnecessary*

stalkette "a female stalker." Other candidates included the euphemism **wardrobe malfunction** "unanticipated exposure of bodily parts (as on television)," and **flip-flopper** "a political candidate who repeatedly reverses positions on important issues."

2005: *Word of the Year* **truthiness** "the quality of stating what one wishes or believes to be true, rather than what one knows to be true"; *Most Useful* **podcast** "a digital feed of audio or video files for downloading to a portable media player"; *Most Creative* **whale tail** "the Y-shaped waistband of a thong or g-string when visible above the waistline of low-riding pants, shorts, or skirts"; *Most Likely to Succeed* **sudoku** "a number puzzle in which numbers 1 through 9 must be placed into a grid of cells so that each row or column contains only one of each number"; *Most Euphemistic* **internal nutrition** "force-feeding a prisoner"; *Least Likely to Succeed* **pope-squatting** "registering a domain name for a new pope before the pope chooses his new name in order to profit from it." Runners-up included **intelligent design** or **ID** "the theory that life could only have been created by a sentient being (promoted by advocates of creation science as a necessary part of school curricula alongside explanations of evolution)," and **muffin top** "the bulge of flesh hanging over the top of low-rider jeans."

2006: *Word of the Year* **to pluto/be plutoed** "to demote or devalue someone"(as happened to the planet Pluto when the International Astronomical Union demoted it from the planet category and renamed it a "dwarf planet"); *Most Useful* **climate canary** "an organism or species whose declining numbers signal an environmental catastrophe caused by climate change"; *Most Creative* **lactard** "a lactose-intolerant person"; *Most Likely to Succeed* **youtube** (verb) "to use the YouTube video website or to place a video on the site"; *Most Euphemistic* **waterboarding** "interrogation technique used on terrorism detainees in which the subject is doused with water to simulate drowning"; *Least Likely to Succeed* **grup** "a Gen-Xer who does not act his or her age" (from an episode of *Star Trek* in which Captain Kirk lands on a planet of children who call Kirk and the crew "grups," which is a contraction of *grown-ups*).

2007: *Word of the Year* **subprime** "adjective describing a risky or less than ideal loan, mortgage, or investment"; *Most Useful* and *Most Likely to Succeed* **green-** "prefix or combining form designating environmental concern, as in *greenwashing*"; *Most Creative* **Googlegänger** "person with your name who shows up when you google yourself"; *Most Euphemistic* **human terrain team** "group of social scientists employed by the U.S. military to serve as cultural advisers in Iraq or Afghanistan"; *Least Likely to Succeed* **strand-in** "a protest duplicating being stranded inside an airplane on a delayed flight."

2008: *Word of the Year* **bailout** "the rescue by the government of companies on the brink of failure"; *Most Useful* **Barack Obama,** both names as combining forms (e.g., *Barackafied, Baracklamation, Obamamania, Obamafy, Obamatopia*); *Most Likely to Succeed* **shovel-ready** "(of an infrastructure project) that can be started quickly when funds become available"; *Most Creative* **recombobulation area** "an area in which airline passengers can get their clothes and belongings in order after passing through security screening"; *Most Euphemistic* **scooping technician** "person whose job is to pick up dog poop"; *Most Unnecessary* **moofing** "from Mobile and Out of Office, meaning working on the go with a laptop and cell phone." Other nominations included **lipstick on a pig** "an adornment of something that can't be made pretty," **long photo** "a video of 90 seconds or less (used by the photo-sharing website Flickr.5)," and **rofflenui,** a blended New Zealand English-Maori word meaning "laughing big," formed from the abbreviation *rofl* ("rolling on the floor laughing") + Maori *nui* ("large, big").

Back in 2000, the ADS not only chose the Word of the Year but also the Word of the Decade, the Word of the Century, and the Word of the Millennium. The Word of the Decade was the *Web*, which beat among others the prefix *e-*, the combining form *Franken-*, the terms *ethnic cleansing* and *senior moment*, and the slangy adverb *way* "very," as in *way cool*. The Word of the Century was *jazz*, which outmatched *DNA*, *media*, *melting pot*, *modern*, *World War*, *cool*, *teenager*, *T-shirt*, and *teddy bear*. The Word of the Millennium was the pronoun *she*, which did not exist in Old English before the year 1000; it replaced *heo*, which was too often confused with *he*. A close runner-up to *she* was *science*, which was borrowed from Latin about 1300.

A Selection of New Words of the 2000–2009 Decade

2000

ad creep, blamestorming, bling (n., v.), bling-bling, blog (v.), blue state, bobo (= bourgeois bohemian), B2B2C (= business-to-business-to-consumer), B2C (= business-to-consumer), camikini (swimsuit), C2C (= consumer-to-consumer), crunk (n.), cyberchondria, cyberchondriac, cybercriminal, demalling, digifeiter (= digital counterfeiter), dotbam, downshifting, dramality, egoboo (= ego boost), electronic paper, e-mentor, Evernet, facemail, functional food, geocache, geocaching, get-rich-click, golden rice, hospitalist, iTunes, investomer, Jappening, lifecaster, lifecasting, lotologist, lotology (collecting lottery tickets), maffluent (= mass affluent), marijuana patch, m-commerce, microchannel, missionware, moletronics, mousetrapping, MSP (music service provider), Netco (= Internet company), nutrigenomics, on-hold (adj.), orphan lot, packet monkey, paper road, pin-drop syndrome, PLUR/plur (peace, love, unity, respect), politainer, pop-under (n., adj.), power center, prayer beeper, prophylactic napping, rave music, red state, retail park, Rio hedge, softphone, speed dating, spillback, streamies, T-commerce, teledensity, TiVo (digital video recorder), two-comma (adj., = 100,000,000), typosquatter, typosquatting, URL

hijacking, v-commerce, weapons-grade, web bug, webjack
(v.), webjacking, welfariat (= welfare proletariat), wiki,
WMWM (white married working mom), work rage, yettie
(young entrepreneurial technocrat)

2 0 0 1

adultescent, alpha girl, alpha pup, AOS (all options stink),
ape diet, belligerati, bigature, bioterrorist, blackonomics,
boomburg, Botox party, brandalism, captcha (challenge-
response test), celebriphilia, cell yell, cocktailian, cyberpark
(science and technology park), Denglish/Denglisch
(= Deutsch-English), dot bomb, DWY (driving while
yakking), edubabble, edubabbler, e-textile, Falloween,
fictomercial, gator (v.), Generation 9/11, globesity,
globophobe, hackint, hiss and tell, honeynet, iPod, IP theft
(= intellectual property theft), Islamofascism, Islamofascist,
job spill, lactivist, meatloaf (unsolicited personal e-mail),
middle youth (period between late twenties and mid
forties), newater (reclaimed water), 9/11 or 9-11, passface
(picture-password), patent troll, piconet (short-range
computer network), potty parity, portafuel, posterization,
posterize, proteome, reggaeton (dance music), scatternet,
steganography, stego (v.), suicide bomber, suicide bombing,
TBTF (too big to fail), text (v.), texting, text messaging,
thresholder (= young adult), unconcession, voken

(= virtual token), wardriving (searching for Wi-Fi
networks by car), Websumer, Websumerism, whack (v.),
whacking (= wireless hacking), whitelist, whitelisting

2002

audioblog, bandit sign, barkitecture, belligerati, big-foot (v.),
bioterrorism, bioterrorist, blogosphere, Bluetooth (short-
distance data transmission), bridezilla, buckraker, buckraking
(raking in money from speechmaking), cinematherapy,
commemorabilia, carnographic, carnography, corpocracy,
cosplay (= costume play), CXO (= Chief Executive Officer),
darknet, diabesity (= diabetic obesity), dumpster diver,
embed (n., v.), embedded, ethical hacker, fauxhemian
(= faux bohemian), food desert, hotelling, i-dotter, ideopolis,
jury nullification, metrosexual, micropolitan, militainment,
Millennial Generation (ca. 1980–2000), moblog (= mobile
blog), neurobabble, neuromarketing, Norovirus, orthorexia,
previvor, privatopia (gated community), purple state, racial
profiling, regift (v., n.), regifter, regime change, retrophilia,
rocketing, sedentary death syndrome, soft power, spave (save
by spending), sudden loss of wealth syndrome, theocon,
theoconservatism, t-crosser, trialogue, vig (= vigorish),
visitability, vlog (= video blog), voicism (discrimination
based on voice), warchalking (chalking up Wi-Fi nodes),
wind farm, word burst

2003

adulticide (= adult insecticide), age heaping, avoision (avoidance/evasion), bioremediation, biostitute, bluejack (v.), bluejacking, bungaloft, BRIC (Brazil, Russia, India, China), celebreality, chairobics, chick flick, Chrismukkah, cocktailian, covert couture, endism, fastpacking, FOIAble (obtainable through the Freedom of Information Act), Generation XL, gossypiboma, glurge, glurgy, hand-me-up, hip-hop hug, jetiquette, LinkedIn, nicotini, manscape (v.), manscaping, militainment (= military entertainment), MOUT (Military Operations in Urban Terrain), nerdistan, pescetarian (fish-eating vegetarian), pescetarianism, potscaping (= pot landscaping), protirement, quirkyalone (n.), reax (= reaction[s]), regreen (v.), reprogenetics, rumint (rumored intelligence), SARS (severe acute respiratory syndrome), shock and awe, skinship, Skype (n., v.), snaparazzi (snapshot photographers), speed dating, Stendhal syndrome, storylining, stroke belt (area of high stroke mortality), studentification, superinfector, supertaster, technoburb, third screen, touron, turducken (turkey-duck-chicken dish), truckonaut, type T personality, video pill, wildfeed

2004

aireoke (= air guitar karaoke), babymoon, carbon-neutral (adj.), celesbian (n., adj.), cell phone lot, chofa (= chair-sofa),

crackberry (addictive BlackBerry-like device), Cryovac (v.),
Digg, digital cammies/digi-cammies, dormcest (dorm +
[in]cest), eventize, fat tax, floortime, frienemy/frenemy,
furkid (= furry pet), gayish, go-bag, Googleable,
grasstops (adj.), hathos (hate pathos), heteroflexible,
hick-hop, hoplophobia, hyperparent, leapling, living
bandage, Menglish, menopot, metacopyright,
microfiction, mongo (objects found in trash), movieoke
(= movie karaoke), nanopublishing, paracopyright,
pareidolia, pluot (plum-apricot hybrid), podcast (v., n.),
podcasting, presidentialness, prevenge, purple state,
ranchburger (cookie-cutter style ranch), retrosexual (n., adj.),
roentgenium, sell-by-date (SBD), sitcomedian, sitcomedy
(= sitcom comedy), smartphone, social network, social
networking, sousveillance, spim (spam via IM), spimmer,
stop-loss (policy, law), supercentenarian, technosexual
(n., adj.), togethering, tweaked (= high on drugs), use-by-date
(UBD), velocitize, voice lift, wardrobe malfunction,
waterboarding, white food, wildcrafting

2005

audioblogging, buildering, cankle (= calf-ankle),
condop (= condo-coop), crisis management, crittercam,
cybervigilante, cybervigilantism, digilantism, domainer,
domaining, flexitarian (= flexible vegetarian), flexitarianism,

folksonomic, folksonomy, freakonomics, freerunning, geekerati, geofence, geofencing, giraffiti (giraffe-high graffiti), hymenoplasty, ICE (In Case of Emergency), IDP (internally displaced person), inshoring, internal nutrition, lawyer up (v.), lifehack, lifehacker, man date, mashup, microvacation, nearshoring, parkour (PK), pedlock (= pedestrian gridlock), permatemp, placemaking, placeshift, placeshifting, podcatcher, podcatching, podjacking (= podcast hijacking), profiler, puggle (= pug-beagle hybrid), reggaeton, rightshoring, rootkit (malware), schwag (promotional item), sideload, sideloading, sphereing, splog (= spam blog), splogger, squick, stop-loss job, stylometrist, sudoku, thumboard, traceur, tweaker, vidcast (= vodcast), videoblogging, viewshaft, vodcast (= video podcast), vodcasting, VoIP (Voice over Internet Protocol), walk-through, white tail, zorb (v.)

2006

architourism, architourist, bacn ("bacon"—unsolicited communication), biodiverse, black site (classified military site), blook (= blog book), boomeritis, cami (= camisole), celebutard (= celebrity retard), Chumby, clickprint, climate canary, crowdsourcing, dwarf planet, ecolonomics (= ecology economics), ego-surfing, elbow bump,

fauxtography, fratire (= fraternity satire), freemium
(= free premium), foreclosureville, gallerist, grup,
gurgitator, Katrina cottage, lactard, lifestreaming, live blog,
live-blog (v.), locavore (= local food eater), lo-fi, ludologist,
ludology, mancation (= male-only vacation), mancursion,
megadiversity, menaissance, murse (= man's purse), office
spouse, pap (v., photograph by paparazzi), pluto (v.), pound
hug (= hip-hop hug), pro-ana (= pro anorexia), pro-mia
(= pro bulimia), ransomware (malware demanding
ransom), rejuvenile (adj.), rejuvenalia, ringtone, ringxiety
(= ringtone anxiety), robocall (automated phone call),
sharrow (arrowlike markings for bicycle route), snowclone
(phrasal cliché), songlifting, springspotter, steez (style with
ease), steezy, stunt casting (of a celebrity), tapafication,
thinspiration, unibrow, UMPC (Ultra-Mobile Personal
Computer), video clip, vishing, vlog, vlogger, Wintel
(Windows on Intel), youtube (v.), zero-day

2007

amigurumi (knitted Japanese doll), barista, BFF
(best friends forever), BOGOF (buy one get one free),
bogotify (make or become bogus), cheat up, collabulary
(= collaborative vocabulary), exergame (= exercise game),
exergaming, exertainment, facebook (v.), fist bump, fixie
(fixed-gear bicycle), floordrobe (= floor wardrobe), freebate

(= free after rebate), freetard (free' + [re]tard), friend (v. = add a friend to a list), gallerist (= gallery owner), genarian (= sexagenarian, septuagenarian, etc.), glamping (= glamorous camping), Globish (= Global English), Gmail/gmail, high-touch (adj.), human terrain team, hypermiler, hypermiling, intensivist, iPhone, Kindle, knuckle bump, knudge, man hug (hip-hop hug), microblogging, mockbuster (blockbuster knockoff), monetize, moofing (= mobile, out of office), netbook, newpeat (= new repeat), pack-year (cigarette smoking measure), plutonomy, poorism, poverty tourism, sheeple (= sheep people), shoefiti (= shoe graffiti), sister-wife (in polygamous marriage), subprime, sungazer, sungazing, strand-in, Tase (v.), texter, TGIM (Thank God It's Monday), truther, upcycling, vacay (= vacation), VBIED (vehicle-borne improvised explosive device), wrap rage (at rigid plastic packaging)

2008

age-doping, agflation (= agricultural inflation), boo (= boyfriend), burqini/burkini (Muslim woman's swimsuit), carborexic (= carbon anorexic), CGI (computer-generated imagery), cupcaking, dap (a fist bump), daycation (= days-off vacation), doomer, DWT (driving while texting), edupunk, elderproof (adj., v.), exoplanet

(= extrasolar planet), facadectomy (façade removal), flirtationship, foodshed, frugalista, game-changer, genopolitics, gold party, homedebtor, hydrail (hydrogen railway), I.E.D. (improvised explosive device), malus (salary cut, opposite of bonus), meetup, mezzanine financing, mezzanine loan, MRSA (Methicillin resistant Staphylococcus aureus), netroots, newb (= newbie), on-ramp (n.), peaknik diaspora (peak oil, peak carbon, peak dollars, etc.), peeps (= people), plutoid, pregorexia, punditariat, recessionista, returnment, scuppie (socially conscious yuppie), shoeing, shovel-ready, skadoosh, slow medicine, smart power, sonopuncture, spec house, squirter (fleeing insurgent), tat (n., v., = tattoo), thinko, third-hand smoke, throwie, thunder thighs, tipping element, transliteracy, trashout, walkshed (walkable area)

2009

bet dieting, Bing, carborexia, car czar (for carmakers' bailout), cookprint, crowd mining, cyberwar, cyberwarfare, e-book, e-book reader (e.g., Kindle), e-cigarette (mixture of nicotine and water vapor), e-smoker, eventize, fat tail (finance), flotsametrics, FSBO (For Sale by Owner), ghost call, green job, hetero hug (= hip-hop hug), hockey mom, homedulgence, H1N1 (swine flu), Idaho stop, kabbalese, KenKen, LGBT (Lesbian, Gay, Bisexual, Transgendered),

Madoffed, mindcasting, mockumentarist, mockumentary, niche dating, noob/n00b/newb (= newbie), octomom, O generation (= Obama generation), Palm Pre (smartphone), p-book (= print book), prebituary, predictive dialing, Primobolan, run-walk (adj., v.), scroogeonomics, self-tracker, self-tracking, slackonomics, SLR (Single-Lens Reflex) camera, slumdog, SMS (Short Message Service), social network/social networking, space headache, staycation/stacation (= stay-at-home vacation), TARP (Troubled Assets Relief Program), titlenomics, 201(k) (a reduced 401(k) retirement account), VB6 (= vegan before 6 P.M.), weisure (= work-leisure blend), womenomics, yogasm (yoga orgasm), ZIRP (Zero Interest Rate Policy)

Conclusion: The New Words Lists

One of the consequences of the great expansion of English vocabulary during the twentieth century was an increased interest in word formation and word study. Competing dictionaries vied for extended coverage of new words and the inclusion of usage notes. Books on usage became popular and influential, from H. W. Fowler's *A Dictionary of Modern English Usage* (1926) and Eric Partridge's *Usage and Abusage* (1942) to Bergen and Cornelia Evans's *A Dictionary of Contemporary American Usage* (1957), Wilson Follett's *Modern American Usage* (1966), William and Mary Morris's *Harper Dictionary of Contemporary Usage* (1975), *Webster's Dictionary of English Usage* (1989), and more recently, Bryan A. Garner's *Garner's Modern American Usage* (2003). Newspaper and magazine columns on usage and style became standard fare for readers both in Britain and America, and since the advent of computers and the Internet such information is literally on the fingertips of millions.

The availability of so much knowledge on the English language and its lexicon has made it possible— almost imperative—to make the point of this book simple and direct, without elaborate explanations. Thus it seemed unnecessary to define individually, as dictionaries do, the terms listed at the end of each chapter under the title "A Selection of New Words of the ___Decade." A great many of the words in these lists, especially those recorded between 1900 and 1950, are familiar to most readers and can be found in standard dictionaries. Those that first appeared after the 1950s are found without much effort on the Internet. Finally, the attentive reader will notice that in many instances, to avoid confusion or ambiguity, I suggest the meaning or etymology of a term by following it with a brief hint in parentheses, e.g., *limbo* (dance), *OD* (= overdose), *faction* (fact + fiction), *bot* (= robot), *QED* (quantum electrodynamics), *Kwanza/ Kwanzaa* (African American festival), *Sally Mae* (SLMA), *at sign* (= @). The Selection of New Words lists are not meant to be all-inclusive, since including thousands of new words would have consumed an inordinate amount of space. On average, five hundred new terms took root in the language every year since 1900, while hundreds more went by the wayside. Among the thousands coined each year, many were technical terms, loanwords, phrases, derived forms, or idiomatic expressions, and those I have excluded for the most part from the Selection of New Words.

How many of the thousands of new coinages that broke into English since 1900 are destined to survive? This question was raised by the American linguist and word authority Allan Metcalf in a fascinating book, *Predicting New Words—The Secrets of Their Success*, published in 2002. Professor Metcalf, executive secretary of the American Dialect Society, had been tracking new words for sixty years and has written extensively about them. Though he makes few direct predictions in his book, he does propose a theory about the chances of a new word to survive. Those chances, he writes, depend on five factors, which he calls the FUDGE factors: Frequency of use; Unobtrusiveness; Diversity of uses and situations; Generation of other forms and meanings; Endurance of the concept. On a scale that allows 0, 1, or 2 for each factor, a total score of 0, 1, or 2 dooms a word to failure, a total score of 4 or 5 gives the word a slim chance of survival, while a total score of 10 makes it a clear winner and likely to endure.

Professor Metcalf's scale is a very useful measure, though he does admit that only time will tell how dependable it is. "Even if a new word or phrase seems spectacularly successful," he writes, "past experience indicates that it will take about two generations, or forty years, to determine whether that word will embed itself in the permanent vocabulary." I fully agree with him that the element of time is crucial in determining a new word's survivability. But I am not persuaded that forty years is enough to declare a winner or loser. There is such a thing as long-term memory. Professor Metcalf cites the word *flapper* from the 1920s and *Castroism, Fidelista, sit-in* (to end racial segregation), and *sex kitten* from the 1960s as words that have failed to take root. However, these words are still part of our collective memory and may come up in conversation or writing at any moment. As long as people will read such classsics as *The Great*

Gatsby, A Farewell to Arms, The Grapes of Wrath, The Catcher in the Rye, and *Fahrenheit 451,* the words of their respective periods will live on. I would suggest waiting a century before pronouncing a word dead, however moribund it may seem at times. Words, like humans, may fall into a comatose or vegetative state, but often speakers or writers with a sense of history will breathe new life into seemingly dead words.

The Internet has also changed the way words live. Whether you cruise the Net on a casual excursion or embark on it in a determined search, you are bound to discover words both long forgotten and of recent coinage. As a repository and preserver of English vocabulary, the Internet and its World Wide Web may ensure the longevity of our words, old and new.

Acknowledgments

In researching this book, I have consulted a variety of sources of information. Among them were the *Barnhart Dictionary of New English* series (1973, 1980, 1990), the *Random House Historical Dictionary of American Slang* (ed. J. E. Lighter, 1994–97), the *Random House Webster's College Dictionary* (2000), and the *Chronology of the 20th Century* (1995, Helicon), by Philip Waller and John Rowett. My primary source for ascertaining the earliest dates of many words has been the invaluable *Oxford English Dictionary Online*, whose treasure-trove of citations covers the entire history of the English language. I also utilized some of the Internet's search engines for verification of dates, names, and other facts that were unavailable in standard reference books.

I am grateful for the support given this project by Tom Russell, publisher of Random House Reference, and Shaye Areheart, publisher of Harmony Books. I especially wish to thank John A. Glusman, vice president and executive editor of Harmony Books, and his outstanding staff, including Anne Berry, Domenica Alioto, Rachelle Mandik, and Laurie McGee, for bringing this work to light.

Index

About the Author

S ol Steinmetz is a well-known lexicographer and the former editorial director of Random House Reference. He has contributed articles to the *Encyclopedia Americana* and *The Oxford Companion to the English Language,* and has been a consultant to the *Encarta World English Dictionary*. He is currently a language consultant to the *Oxford English Dictionary*. His books include *Semantic Antics: How and Why Words Change Meaning*; *The Life of Language: The Fascinating Ways Words Are Born, Live & Die*; *Dictionary of Jewish Usage: A Guide to the Use of Jewish Terms*; *Youthopia USA*; *Mshuggenary*; and *The Story of Yiddish in America*.